How to FART at School...

Published in 2012 by Prion
an imprint of the Carlton Publishing Group
20 Mortimer Street
London W1T 3JW

10 9 8 7 6 5 4 3 2 1

Copyright © 2012 Carlton Books Limited

This book is sold subject to the condition that it shall not, by way of trade or otherwise, be lent, resold, hired out or otherwise circulated without the publisher's prior written consent in any form of cover or binding other than that which it is published and without a similar condition, including this condition, being imposed upon the subsequent purchaser. All rights reserved.

ISBN 978-1-85375-872-0

Project Editor: Richard Wolfrik Galland
Editor: Lesley Malkin
Designer: Claire Cater
Illustrations: Chris Gould
Production: Dawn Cameron

A CIP catalogue record of this book can be obtained from the British Library.

Printed and bound in Great Britain by CPI Group (UK) Ltd, Croydon CR0 4YY

How to FART at School...

...and get away with it!

Adrian Besley

Introduction

School can be a be a dull place (unless you're a swot or teacher's pet) so every now and then someone has to step up and break the boredom.

That's where you come in.

Nothing improves a boring lesson like a well-timed fart or a hilarious practical joke. Whether you are being Super Farter or The Pranksterman, you'll be the superhero of the school, president of the playground and captain of the corridor — they might even award you a special prize at the end-of-term assembly (although don't hold your breath waiting for this one.)

This book is your guide to brightening a boring class, packing break times with laughs, causing chaos in assembly and generally making mayhem throughout the school. It'll show you how, when and where to explode your bottom bombs and give you a load of pranks that hopefully won't land you in a whole heap of trouble (no promises though!). Each farty-licious trick has a 'report card' that will grade you prankster performance if you manage to pull it off. You can keep track of your 'prank points' at the end of the week using the score card on page 144.

WARNING These tricks, games and pranks can be dangerous in the wrong hands so use them wisely. Is your teacher going red in face and muttering to himself? Time to leave him alone if only for your own safety. Have you made one kid the target of your pranks one time too many? Lay off him, and find another target – it's much funnier to spread the laughs around. Is there a letter to your parents from the Head? You might have taken things a bit too far...
Remember to treat your classmates the way you would want to be treated.
The publisher takes no responsibility for your behaviour.

Contents

Pranksters Paradise 8
   Teachers 10
Friends 11
   Enemies 12
The School Assembly 14
   Bubble Wrap 16
Charity Fartathon 18
   Cup o' Fart 20
Doorknob 22
   An 'A' in Farting 24
Fart Chase 26
   The Fart Fairy 28
Fart in a Jar 30
   The Fart Machine 32
Fart or Dare 34
   The Fart Pact 36
Poetry Corner 38
   Fart Ventriloquism 40
Have you got the X-Farter? 42
   How to Armpit Fart 44
Library Time 46
   Good Morning Bottom 48
No Escape 50
   Parent's Evening 52
Pull My Finger 54
   The Queue Buster 56
The School Play 58
   Schools Out! 60
Silent But Deadly 62
   The Sporting Fart 64
Submarine 66
   Talking Bottoms 68
The School Bus 70

The Swimming Pool	72
You Said "Fart"!!	74
How Loud Can You Go?	76
Fart Spotting	78
Do the Splits	80
What Time is it?	82
Door Ambush	84
Empty Room	86
Hide and Don't Seek	88
Hands Full	90
I ♥ Teacher	92
Lost in the Toilet Paper Factory	94
The Magic Spot	96
On the Money	98
Packed-Back Backpack	100
Pin the Glass	102
A Curious Class	104
Sticky Note Car	106
Finger in a Cup	108
Shoelacing!	110
Snake in the Class	112
Squirty Time	114
Table of Water	116
The Magic Word	118
The Name Switch	120
The Sound of Music	122
Minty Teeth	124
Timber!	126
Kick Me!	128
Yum, Yum, Wiggly Worm!	130
You Spilled What?	132
Your Shoes Are Too Small	134
Cactus Friend	136
Binocular Eyes	138
This Takes the Biscuit	140
Chicken Run	142

Prankster's Paradise!

Your school. You have to go so you might as well have some fun. This is where you will perform your magnificent farts and tricks. The school is your theatre, your stage, your stadium and your arena. But an important part of your art will be deciding which prank to perform, and where...

The Classroom
This is where you and your classmates spend the day cooped up but it is also your domain. You have all the necessary knowledge to pull off a great prank. You know who sits where, what's kept where and, most importantly, the quickest way out of the room.

> **Good because...** You have a 'captive' audience – they (even the teacher!) are unable to escape no matter how much you embarrass them, irritate them or stink them out with a real cheesy bum-cracker!

> **Bad because...** It won't take long for them all to have you marked down as Number One Mischief-Maker. You'll lose the element of surprise and the accusing finger will point your way when anyone lets loose even the smallest of bottom burps.

The Playground
This is where you can escape the beady eye of the teachers to plan and execute your best pranks. Run your games and competitions at break times and use any secret hiding places to perform the pranks that you wish to keep secret.

> **Good because...** You have a brilliant opportunity to choose your victims, anyone from playground assistants to the kids in other years. Plan it right and you can prank five or more kids in one break.

> **Bad because...** Fresh air is the farter's biggest enemy. It is too easy for a perfect stinker to float off in the air without anyone catching a whiff.

The Canteen

Lunchtime. Perfect. The dinner ladies and chefs are super busy, your audience are relaxing with their food and drink... It's Showtime!

Good because... Cups, water, plates, tables are all easily available. It's as if someone's prepared the stage for you!

Bad because... Where there's food, drink and masses of kids, there are going to be farts galore. Can you get your buttock-boilers to stand out from the crowd?

The School Toilets

An ideal place to perform some of your pranks without being disturbed by an angry teacher. Beware though, getting caught in the girls' toilets if you are a boy (or the other way round), is going to land you right in a proper stink.

Good because... It's the natural home for a Superfarter like you!

Bad because... Let's be honest here. Other kids' farts smell pretty awful compared with your bottom concoctions, don't they?

Teachers

Mean, vindictive, bullying slave drivers — and that's just the nice ones! Even your most fun teacher is not going to want to see you farting and pranking all day long — they seem to think school is for other stuff. Know your teacher. Perhaps she is a nervous supply teacher just waiting to be pranked, or have you been lumbered with the snarling, bad-tempered strict sort who thinks he is still in the army? The Super prankster will need to out-smart them all, know how far he can push them until they explode with frustration and rage — and most of all, avoid that dreaded trip to the Head's office!

Friends

All pranksters need their besties. Ideally you'll have one who is almost as clever as you. He can plan your tricks and games with you, and help out when you need an assistant. He too can let rip with a wicked bottom-brew and lie through his teeth to help you out of trouble. On the other hand, it's also helpful to have a bestie who's — how would you say it — not quite so bright. You can practise your tricks on him and know he'll enjoy it no matter smelly and wet he ends up being, or how foolish he looks.

Enemies

Anyone is fair game for your pranks but it's good to pick someone who needs a lesson... in fun.

The Bully

He swaggers around like he owns the school and everyone is scared of him. But wouldn't it be great to bring him down to size with a well-timed prank? You'll be the class hero!
Just don't let him find out that you were the mastermind behind his latest humiliation.

The Swot

If he was as intelligent as he claims, he'd never fall for your tricks. While he's waving his hand in the air desperate to answer every question or has his head in a book, you can devise a prank that will make him look a lot less clever.

Mr Popular
He's the school sports star and seems to get top grades without even trying. The younger kids hero-worship him and, for some reason, all the girls have his name scrawled on their pencil cases. He still hasn't learned that no one is too cool to be pranked.

Little Miss Perfect
Grrrrr! She never has a hair out of place or even the tiniest stain on her clothes. She's first to hand in her homework and last to leave the class because she's helping teacher carry his books. Nothing bad ever happens to Little Miss Perfect, unless…

The Rival
It isn't easy being the King of Pranks. There's always someone trying to knock you off your throne. You need to be alert to see what kind of tricks your rival is up to, be careful not to fall into their traps – and grab any opportunity to make them the victim of your next trick.

The School Assembly

Make two hundred kids giggle like mad – with just one bottom blast.

- Sometimes it's better to stay undetected when you create a super-stinker. The school assembly is just such an occasion.

- Assemblies are so boring. Even though they have to put up with an unpleasant smell, most kids will be grateful for a laugh while the Head is droning on and on.

- Be careful when you are in a long assembly. If you get a 'numb bum' (when you've been sitting for so long you can hardly feel it) you might lose control and let a valuable fart out by accident.

Wait for your perfect moment. When the year three recorder recital has ended or just as the Head reads out the latest terrible football result. That's the time to really let one fly. A fart that can be heard all around the room. Watch with pride, but keep your head down as the whole school falls into hysterics and the teachers angrily try to find the culprit.

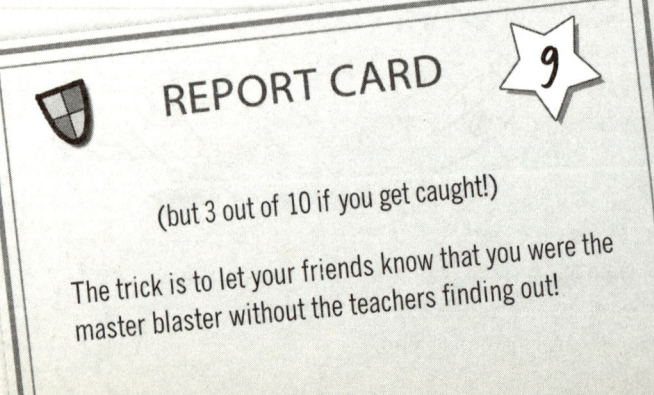

REPORT CARD 9

(but 3 out of 10 if you get caught!)

The trick is to let your friends know that you were the master blaster without the teachers finding out!

Bubble Wrap

What's that sound? Surely not? Little Miss Perfect is going fart crazy!

You've had enough of being told that your brilliant bottom burps are disgusting. It's time a certain little princess was taught a lesson!

- Keep a watch on the girls' toilet. When it's empty, leave a guard on the door to make sure you are not interrupted.

- You need to work fast. Take a piece of bubble-wrap and fold it over twice. Use some sticky tape to stick it to the underside of the toilet seat (a dirty job but someone has to do it!) and repeat with two other pieces.

- Retreat to a safe distance where you can keep an eye on who is entering the toilet. When she enters a cubicle, make sure as many kids as possible are in a position to hear.

As soon as she sits down you should hear a cascade of popping noises – pretty much like you-know-whats! And the laughs of her 'audience' will make sure she knows that everyone is listening.

REPORT CARD

A trick that is full of danger. Get caught in the girls' loo and you'll be in big trouble. But is it worth it to see Little Miss Perfect getting flustered and pink in the cheeks? It sure is!

Charity Fartathon

"But Miss, it's for a good cause!"

You can dress up in silly costumes, have a bath in baked beans, throw wet sponges at the teachers in the name of charity – so why not do what you do best: fart to help others?

- Next time one of the big charity days comes round at school, it's your turn to be the star money raiser.

- Ask people to agree to pay you a certain amount of money for every fart you can produce on that day.

- Get your one of your besties to be your witness. He must be at your side everywhere you go in the day – even, and especially, to the loo.

- He should note down every fart you do and count up the total at the end of the day. The following day you can collect the promised money and proudly present it to the Head as your contribution to the charity.

 REPORT CARD

Who can complain as you put your farting skills to a good cause? The more farts you do, the more money you collect – brilliant! This might turn out to be the only day that Little Miss Perfect applauds every sound emerging from your backside.

Cup o' Fart

"What are you holding there? Show us, go on, show us.... Euuugghhhhhhh!"

- If there's one thing that's disappointing about a bottom burp – it's that the fun is gone almost as soon as it's left your butt. Nothing is worse when you've delivered the perfect fart than to realize that no one was around to witness its awesome aroma. What you need is Cup o' Fart, the ideal means of transporting a super-stinker.

- You don't need a real cup, just cup your hands together and position them under your bum. Keep your hands closed, tightly but gently – as if you had caught a butterfly. You now have about a minute to use your fart grenade.

- Use it wisely. You could ask people to guess what you have in your hands (although if you've a reputation – they might just work it out!), surprise the girls in their skipping game or, most disgusting of all, sneak up behind a friend and open it out in his face – uuugh!!

- Now, you might want to wash your hands.

REPORT CARD

Play this trick successfully just once and you'll be able to use it forever. Want to scare someone away? Just cup your hands. They won't know if there's a smell inside or not – but who wants to take the risk?

Doorknob

Doorknob is a game that brings chaos to a classroom in seconds. At the slightest sound of a backside parp, the farter desperately heads for the nearest door and the rest of the class tries to stop him. There are just a few rules...

- Everyone in the class is included in the game whether they like it or not.

- At the sound of even the quietest fart, the bottom bugler must shout "Safety" before anyone else cries "Doorknob!"

- If the "Doorknob" cry sounds out first, the farter must touch the doorknob or handle before he can call "Safety" again.

- Before he gets there, everyone else can poke or tickle him (note: no punches or kicks allowed – they hurt!)

- This game is especially good in the playground or on the sports field when there isn't a door for miles!

REPORT CARD

Farting, uproar and laughs – a fabulous game for the whole class. You deserve a bonus point if you can convince your teacher that it has fitness benefits.

An 'A' in Farting

The test is on – the concentration, the tension, the silence – you just know what's going to happen... pffffftttttttttt!

- It's so quiet you can hear the clock clicking and The Swot's pencil going scratch, scratchy, scratch. But there's one thing on everyone's mind – not who's going to do the best in the test, but who's going to break the silence with a real belter.

- Usually your best farting efforts are drowned out by screeching chairs, teachers shouting and general classroom cacophony. But in the silence of a test even the quietest parp can be appreciated by everyone in the room.

- Worried about coming bottom of the class? Never fear. Try to sit next to The Swot. Not to copy their answers, but to make sure you put them off when you drop an atomic bottom bomb.

- Best of all, the teacher isn't going to want to spoil the chances of his class doing well by bawling you out in the middle of the test. If he grabs you afterwards, just say the nerves got to you and it just slipped out.

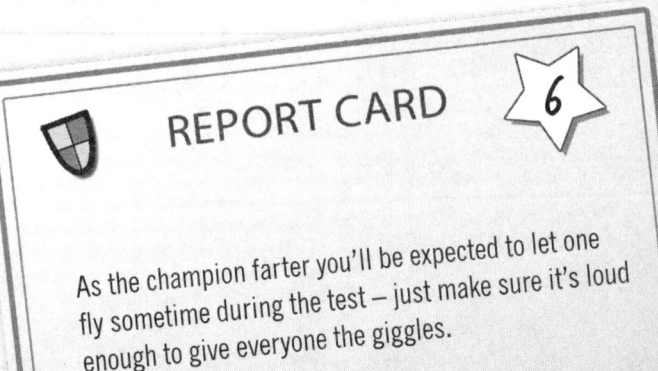

REPORT CARD 6

As the champion farter you'll be expected to let one fly sometime during the test – just make sure it's loud enough to give everyone the giggles.

Fart Chase

You've been cooped up in class all morning – but at last it's break! Now you can get some fresh air and release some epic farts. Why not use them as part of your fun? It's time for the best playground game ever!

- This game is basically the same as 'it' or 'tag' except for one difference. You've guessed it – fart power!

- Select one person who is 'it'. They stay as 'it' until they can hand it over to someone else.

- To pass the fart you have to stand next to your victim, fart and shout (in case they didn't hear it) "Blat!"

- Returns are allowed – if you can fart straight back at them, they are 'it' again. This can go on until one of you runs out of gas!

- The game can go on in class or in playground and continue over a number of break times.

- You might find no-one wants to hang around you when you are 'it'. But they'll forget in the end and then, when they are least suspecting: "Blat!" – you got them!

 REPORT CARD

This is more difficult than it looks. Try running after a friend and not letting a bottom burp slip out! But with a playground full of farters, it's the best game ever!

The Fart Fairy

But you really have to believe...

Do you still believe in the tooth fairy? Or are you just pretending so you can get some money out of your parents? If there are kids in your class who believe in fairies, tell them about this one. The Fart Fairy, who appears and grants you a wish whenever you fart three times in a row.

Ok. There really is no such thing. But why should that mean you miss out on some fun. You and your friends can still all agree that three guffs on the trot means the Fart Fairy gives you star status. For a day, you get to be King. You can agree on exactly what that means but it could include:

- Being allowed to wear the 'Star Farter' badge.

- Everyone has to bring you some sweets in the morning.

- You get to go to the front of the dinner queue.

- You get to be captain and have first pick when you are next choosing teams.

- You get to choose which prank the gang play next.

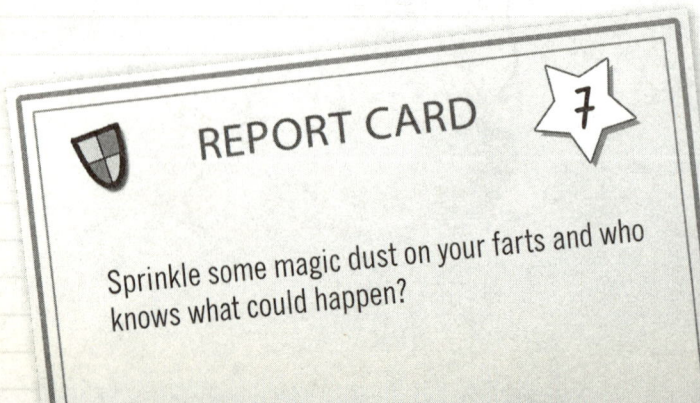

REPORT CARD 7

Sprinkle some magic dust on your farts and who knows what could happen?

Fart in a Jar

Does this ever happen to you? You're sitting in the bath at home or lying on your bed and let rip with the greatest fart ever – the noise bounces off the walls and the smell fills the air in seconds. It's so sad that you're the only one to witness it, but there is a way you can share the thrill...

- You'll need an air-tight jar – but make sure it's not still smelling of peanut butter or marmite. Hold the lid in one hand and the jar against your bum with the other. When the rear-end rocket lifts-off make sure it heads straight into the jar and slam the lid shut as quick as you can.

- Better still, if you are in the bath capture some of the bubbles that emerge when you fart underwater. These are even more potent, the bubbles help preserve the smell even more.

- Now you can take your jar in to school with you. What's wrong with carrying an empty jar around? You can even pretend that it's a science experiment.

- Wait for your moment and open the lid and release the fart. They should still be pretty whiffy even after a couple of days.

REPORT CARD

Now you need never be without a fart again. And, if you get some real stinkers – maybe you can even sell them and earn some extra pocket money.

The Fart Machine

There are days when even a Master Farter can't summon one up

OK. Let's be honest. Using a fart machine is definitely cheating... but only if you get caught! The fart machine is an electronic means of producing a classic fart sound. There are loads of different ones available in the shops. You can usually choose from at least four different disgusting sounds and they can sometimes be pretty loud too!

- Rule number one. Don't get caught. Operate the machine from inside your pocket or under the desk. Your reputation will be ruined if your friends (and enemies) realize you can't actually fart whenever you want.

- Pick your moment to use the machine. Just as Little Miss Perfect has read her latest beautiful poem to the class or when the teacher bends down to pick up a pen.

- Best of all, buy a fart machine that is operated by remote control. Place the speaker somewhere out of sight but where it can be heard – like behind a curtain or hidden by a bag. Now you can have all kinds of fun pressing the button as your enemies walk by.

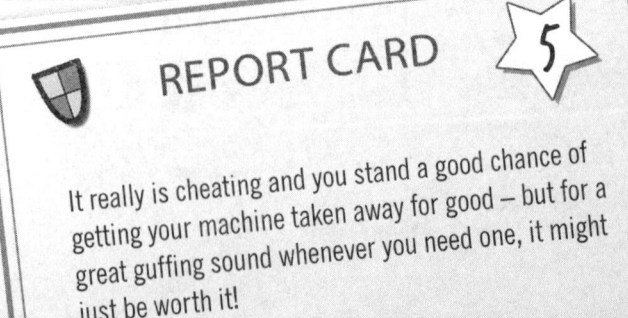

REPORT CARD 5

It really is cheating and you stand a good chance of getting your machine taken away for good – but for a great guffing sound whenever you need one, it might just be worth it!

Fart or Dare

Your parents probably played Truth or Dare when they were at school. You had to either answer an embarrassing question honestly or perform a daring feat. Well, a super-farter isn't interested in the truth, he wants... farts.

- First agree a dare among your gang – something that'll get everyone laughing or embarrass the loser – like running around the playground with your trousers down or writing to a girl to say you love her.

- You've got the rest of the lunchtime to let one fly – at least two people have to witness the bottom explosion – hearing or smelling can both count.

- Anyone who hasn't dropped a stinker by the time the bell goes is the loser and must pay the forfeit.

- If more than two of you fail to produce the goods – arrange a sudden-death fart-off in the afternoon break.

- Once you have a loser, they have a day to perform their dare. Get the whole class – or school – ready to ensure their total humiliation.

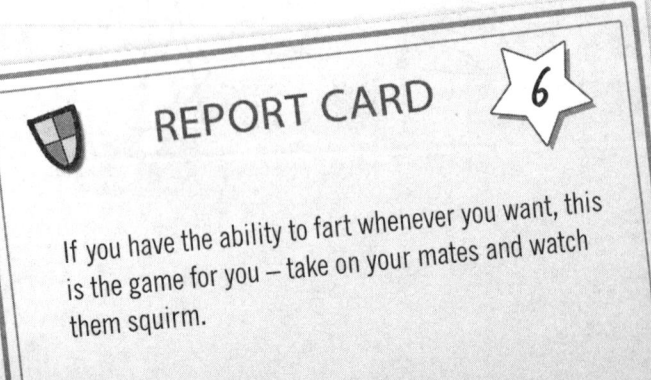

REPORT CARD

6

If you have the ability to fart whenever you want, this is the game for you – take on your mates and watch them squirm.

The Fart Pact

It's time to for a (temporary) truce with your rival. For this prank you are going to need her, and everyone else's, help. Together the two of you can lead a mass fart-a-long that will bring the whole class together.

- To begin with you need to bring together the best farters in the class – even if they are not best friends.

- Agree a time for a mass fart. Three o'clock is an ideal time as it gives your lunch a chance to get some bottom gas going.

- No matter what else is happening – a maths test, a great bit in the story, a recorder recital – as soon as the clock strikes three o'clock, the farters should go into action, encouraging others to do the same.

- The teacher won't know what's happened. One moment, she'll be happily talking and the next the room will be swept by a tidal wave of bad air.

REPORT CARD

As near to perfect as it gets. A class united by the fart – and nobody can blame just you. As the room fills with an unbearable mix of smells from a variety of bottoms – you might even all get sent out to the playground for some fresh air.

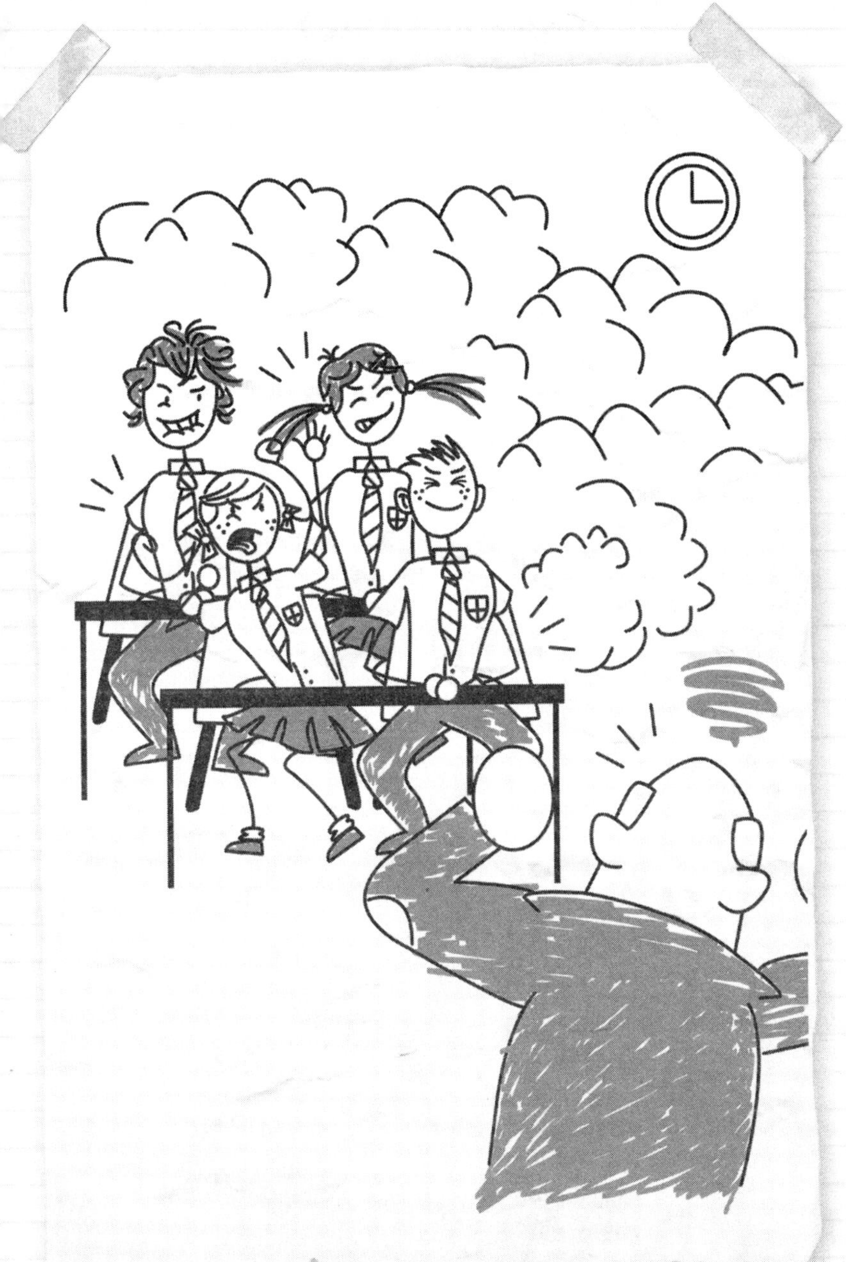

Poetry Corner

Little Miss Perfect and The Swot are forever writing poems about flowers, trees and the sea. How about writing one with a proper subject: the Fart. Here's one to inspire you...

Beans, beans, the musical fruit:
The more you eat, the more you toot!
The more you toot, the better you feel,
So let's have beans for every meal!

Beans, beans, my lunchtime friend
The more you eat, the bigger the wind,
The bigger the wind, the sooner it's passed,
So lift up your leg and let one blast!

Beans, beans, they're good for your heart
The more you eat, the more you fart
I ate my beans and they were loaded,
Went to class and they exploded!

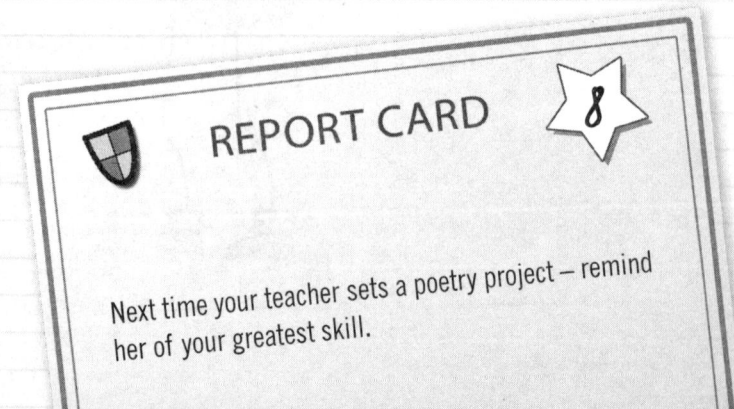

REPORT CARD

Next time your teacher sets a poetry project – remind her of your greatest skill.

39

Fart Ventriloquism

Ventriloquism. It's a difficult word to say and spell and even more difficult to perform. It involves convincing an audience that your voice is actually coming from somewhere else – such as a dummy, puppet or even from inside a box. Luckily, fart ventriloquism is a little easier – no one can see that the noise is coming from your backside.

You'll need a good dummy. Pick your biggest soft toy – you know, the one you hug every night in bed even though you hide it when your friends come round!

When you are ready for a performance, introduce your 'friend' to the audience. Pick a funny name like 'Fartbum the Ferret' or 'Guffo the Farting Lion'.

- Ask your dummy a question. It can be anything from "What do you think of our teacher?" to "Have you anything to say to the boys and girls?"

- Move the dummy's head to look at you and then the audience. Then, lift the dummy's bum a little and let rip with as loud a fart as you can manage. The audience will be in heaps of laughter – guaranteed. If you can manage another question and answer you'll get double the laughter.

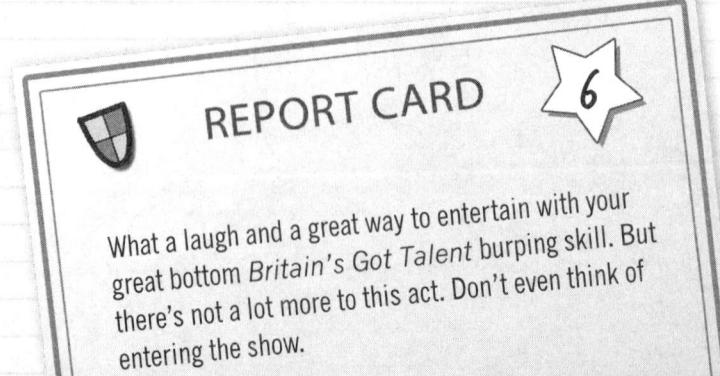

REPORT CARD ☆ 6

What a laugh and a great way to entertain with your great bottom *Britain's Got Talent* burping skill. But there's not a lot more to this act. Don't even think of entering the show.

41

Have you got the X-Farter?

We all want to show off our skills. Some dance, some sing, some perform tricks and, well, some fart. But who has that star quality to make the big time? It's time to find out...

- You'll need to advertise your fart competition. Put a sign up or get everyone to pass the message on in the playground.

- Choose four judges. Make sure they are different kinds of kids – even Little Miss Perfect and The Swot can get involved. Try to get an expert on your panel like they do on the TV shows – someone who really knows his farts.

- Make scorecards from 1 to 6 on pieces of paper and give them to your judges. Keep them small so they can carry them around in their pockets.

- Anyone who has one brewing should be able to summon at least two of the judges and perform their rear-end show in front of them.

- The judges will need to give marks for smell, noise and pure star quality. They should then all hold up their numbers at the same time and an official scorer add up the total points.

- At the end of the day – the week or even the term – the winner can be proclaimed and crowned the school King (or Queen) of Farts.

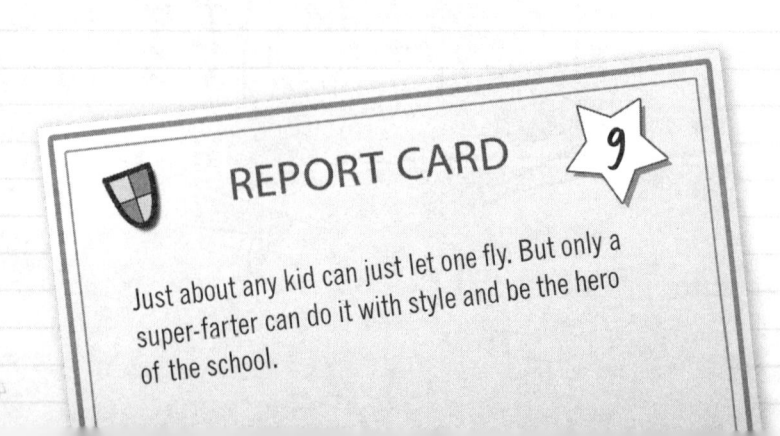

REPORT CARD 9

Just about any kid can just let one fly. But only a super-farter can do it with style and be the hero of the school.

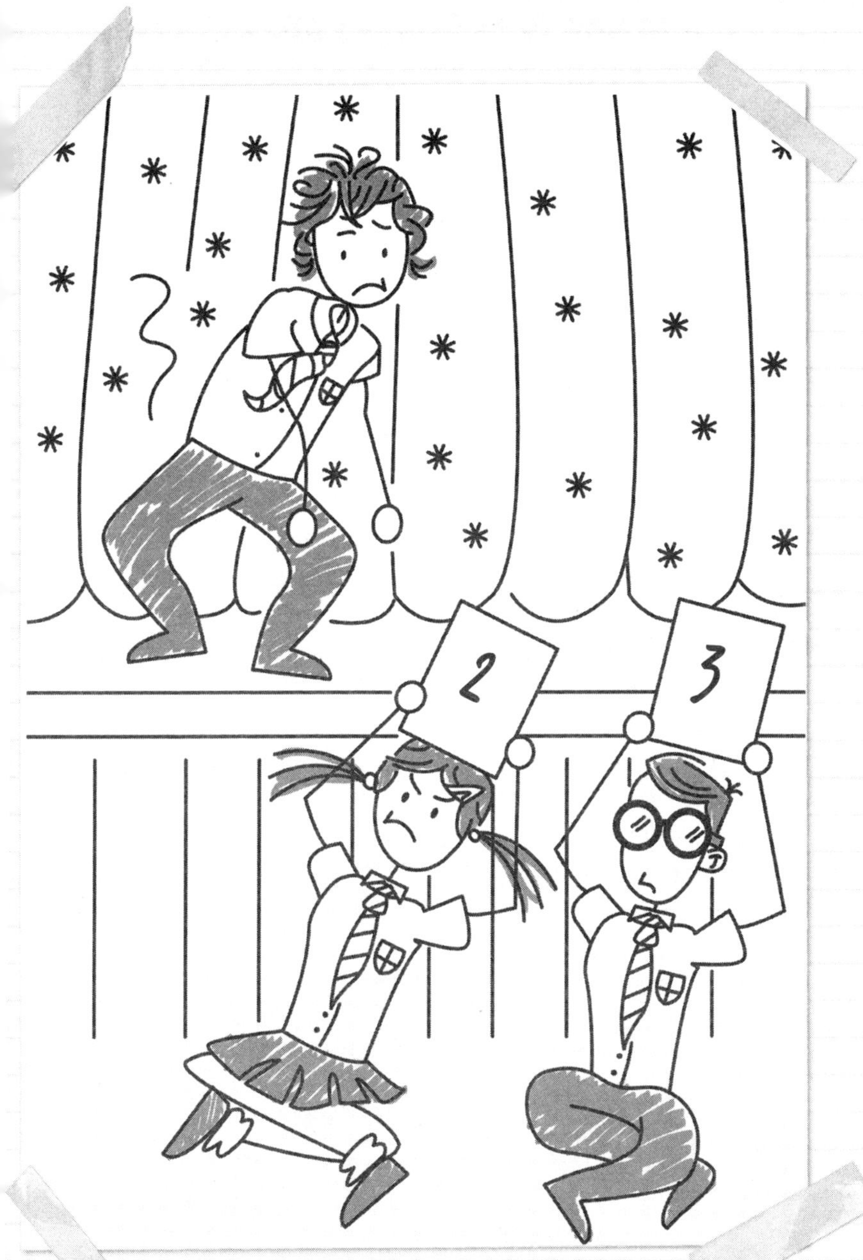
2
3

How to Armpit Fart

A fart with no smell? You might think that's a bit like a Big Mac without a burger or a football match without a ball. What's the point? And you'd be right. Except there are times when this skill is very useful. Like when you want to pretend you've farted, or when you just can't summon one up when it's needed.

So here's how you do it...

- If you are right-handed, make a cup of your left hand. Keep it tight as if you have water in it that you don't want to spill.

- Raise your right hand as if you are asking a question in class.

- Tuck your cupped hand under your shirt and into the hollow of your armpit.

- Grip the edge where the armpit meets your back with your fingers and place your thumb on the front of your shoulder.

- Bring your arm down with a jerk as if you are a chicken flapping its wing.

- You should produce a great farting noise, but you may need a little practice to get it perfect.

REPORT CARD 6

Almost as good as the real thing. The sound can be close enough to fool even a Professor of Farting!

45

Library Time

Shhhhhh... It's the quietest room in the school. There's nobody running around, shouting or scraping chairs on the floor. Just total silence – the perfect place for a real rip-snorter!

- It's the one room in the school where you really shouldn't fart. But who can resist? But the secret here is to wait for your moment.

- Let the class get settled into the library. Allow everyone to choose their books and to get comfortable on the cushions.

- Find yourself a good position. If possible sit down behind a bookshelf where the teacher can't see you.

- Start reading your book. Read a few pages and then have a look around. Is everyone concentrating on their stories? Is the teacher looking the other way? If so, now is the time to let rip.

- Parrrappppppph! Your fart will be all the more impressive for breaking the silence. Make it loud enough and it will echo around the room and reduce the class to a fit of giggles.

- While all around descends into mayhem, put your head straight back in your book. When the teacher looks your way you should look like you are so caught up in your book that you never even noticed that anyone parped.

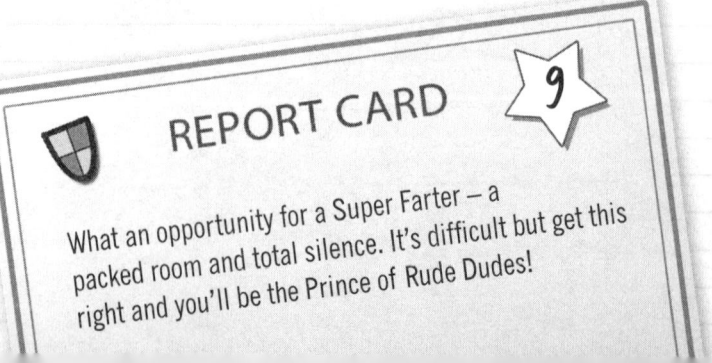

REPORT CARD ⭐9

What an opportunity for a Super Farter – a packed room and total silence. It's difficult but get this right and you'll be the Prince of Rude Dudes!

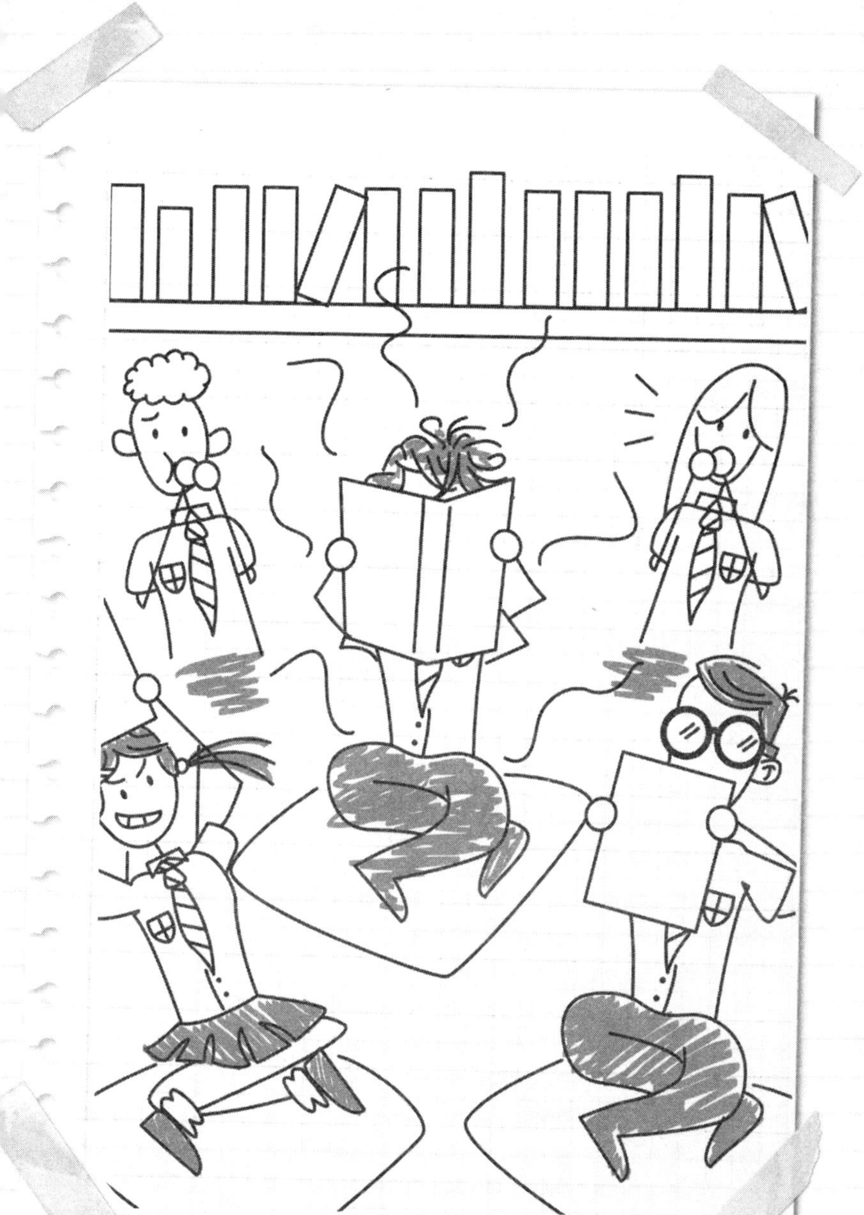

Good Morning Bottom!

Say hello to a brand new day by letting out a breakfast belter – in the school queue...

- Some children wait for the morning register to say "Here, Miss!" but you don't need to wait until then. You can announce your arrival before you even get into the classroom.

- After a good breakfast, you should have a rumbling in the rear ready to make it's explosive appearance. But keep it in for a minute or two.

- When you hear the school bell or whistle make your way to your class queue as normal. Have a glance along the line and see if you can take a place next to your chosen victim.

- If your teacher makes you stand next to the same kid every morning they will soon be dreading the morning queue. Within a week they will be begging to change places.

- Wait for everyone to be in place and the teacher to have control of the line for your rear-end rumpus to cause maximum chaos. Leave it too late and you'll have wasted a precious fart – to stink out an empty playground.

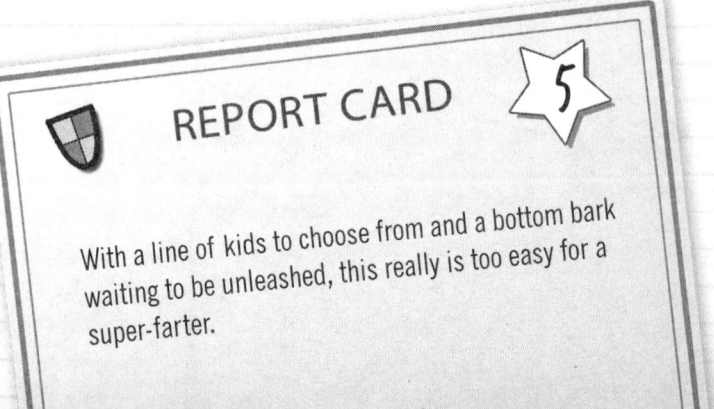

REPORT CARD 5

With a line of kids to choose from and a bottom bark waiting to be unleashed, this really is too easy for a super-farter.

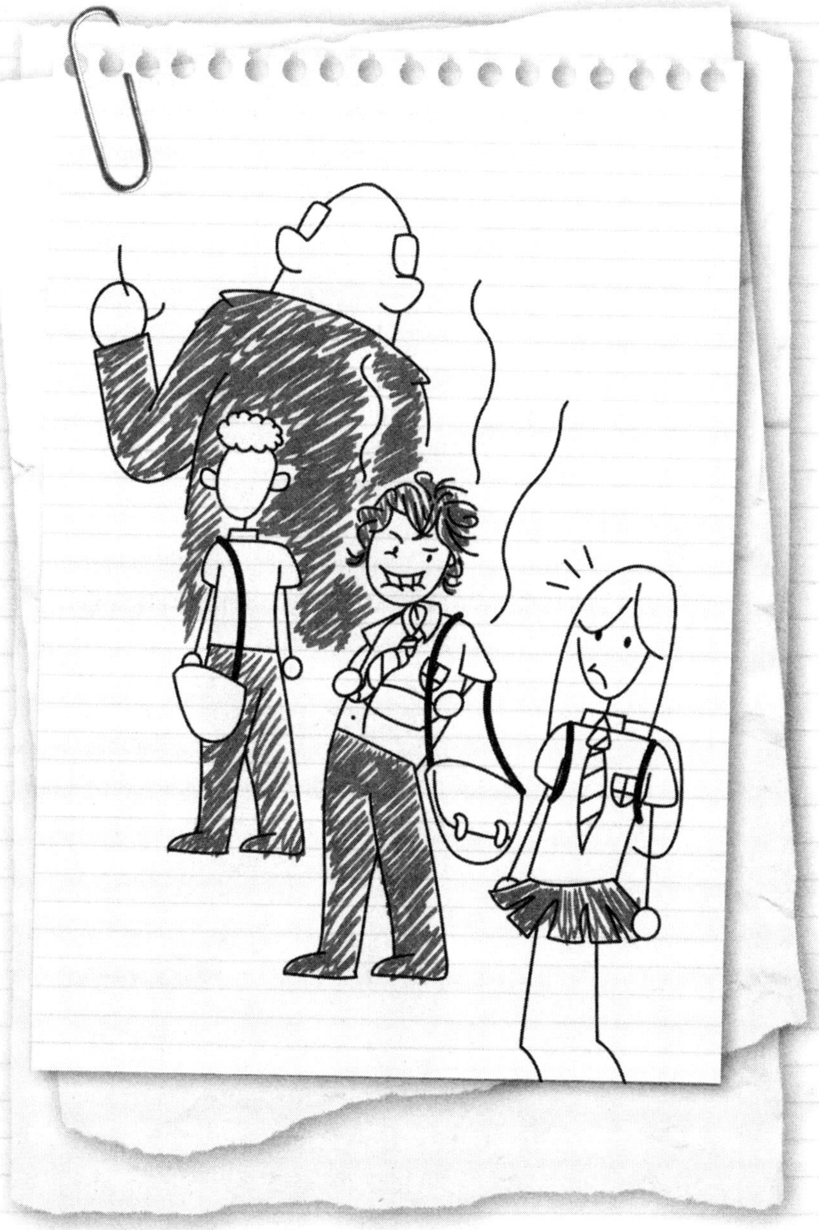

No Escape!

Your teacher is about to start a class. Perhaps it's a literacy lesson, but the most boring time of the day is definitely starting. Unless the Fart Master (that's you!) has been up to his tricks...

- Everyone is going to be stuck in class for a while. This is the perfect time to share your stinkers.

- Take a little walk around the classroom while everyone else is settling down. No one will notice. Little Miss Perfect will be showing the teacher the lovely leaf she found at break.

- As you move around keep letting a fart out every few seconds. Save some really big ones for where your sworn enemies sit.

- Return to your own seat acting as normally as you can. See if you can get the teacher to see you sitting down nicely.

- Wait for the fun to begin.

You will soon hear the cries go up, "Pwoarrr!" as the kids get a sniff of your 'bombs'. They might try to move away but they'll only walk straight into the next one.

There is no escape! Soon there will be chaos all around. As they start accusing each other be sure to join in and lay the blame clearly on your sworn enemy.

REPORT CARD

You'll need to be clever and full of farts to pull off this smelly prank. If all goes to plan it can lead to complete chaos and you won't even get the blame!

51

Parent's Evening

Your parents and your teacher. These are the people you really, really don't want to meet each other. And yet, they arrange a special evening when they do just that – and then they talk about you – the cheek of it!

- Remember, you have one weapon they are all afraid of. We're talking about your humdinger bumslinger! Use it wisely and you can keep the damage to a minimum.

- Listen to what the teacher is saying. If he starts to say anything bad about you then drop a smelly silent one as a warning to him to stop.

- Look as innocent as possible. Grown-ups get incredibly embarrassed when anyone farts. They immediately imagine that everyone will think they have done it.

- If the teacher wants to talk about your farting, they will find it very difficult and refer to "tummy troubles", "excess wind", "passing gas". Look as though you really have no idea what they could be talking about.

- If they force you to say anything, say that you get very nervous in class and sometimes they just slip out – especially if you've had some of the beans they make you eat for lunch!

- Be prepared to end their meeting with a real stinker. Drop one that is so bad that no one can bear to sit at the table any more.

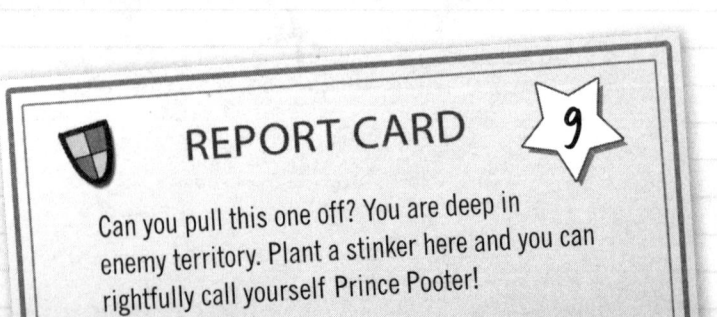

REPORT CARD 9

Can you pull this one off? You are deep in enemy territory. Plant a stinker here and you can rightfully call yourself Prince Pooter!

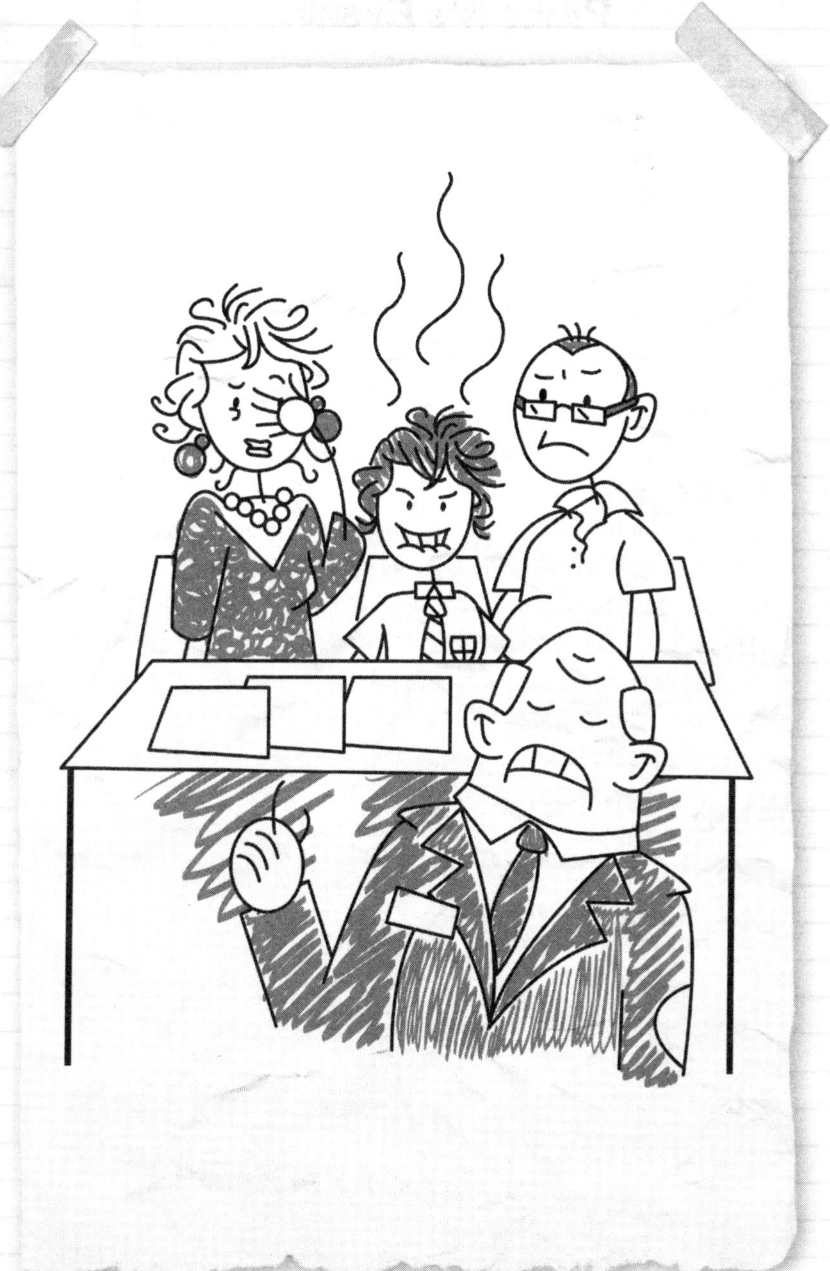

Pull My Finger

Can someone make you fart simply by giving a sharp tug on your middle finger. No, of course not. But it can be great fun to make it seem like it. Next time you've got a real hot bottom bugle ready, stick your finger out and call out to a friend, "Hey! Pull my finger…"

- When they grab it, hopefully not too hard, immediately let one fly as loudly as you can.

- Soon all your mates will be at it. Then the fun comes with waiting for what will happen. Will you get a big cheer for a mighty barrage or be booed for a pathetic pop?

- Now approach Little Miss Perfect, who hasn't seen the trick. She'll be suspicious but persuade her that she'll come to no harm. She won't, but she won't half be surprised when she pulls one end of you and an unpleasant noise emerges from the other!

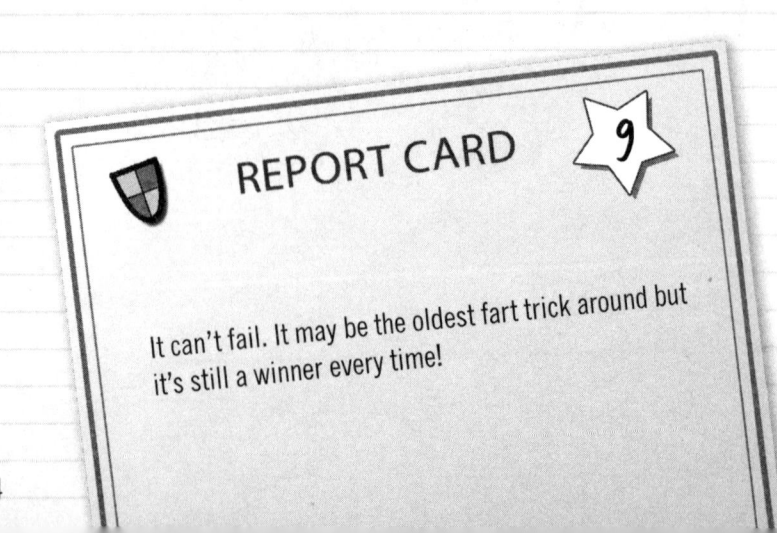

REPORT CARD 9

It can't fail. It may be the oldest fart trick around but it's still a winner every time!

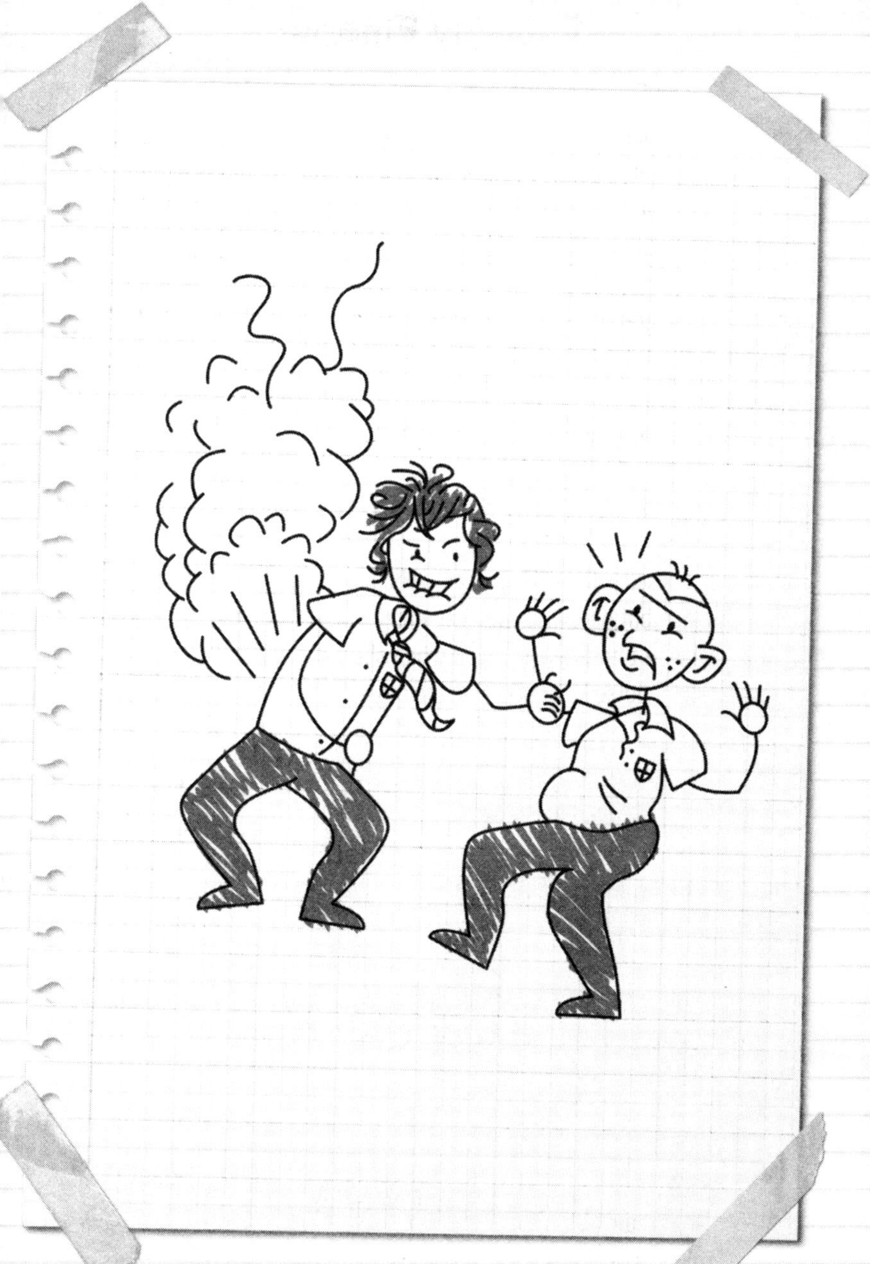

The Queue Buster

"OK 4B, form a line, in twos now, hurry up!" Sometimes it seems you spend half your school life getting in a line. Lines to go in class, lines to go to swimming, lines to go to lunch... It's soooo boring! Unless, of course, you are the phantom farter of the class. In which case it is a wonderful opportunity to create some mayhem.

- This challenge is a battle. It's you against the teacher. They will want a well-behaved straight line. You will be trying to break up the queue as much as possible. Let's see who wins...

- Let the teacher think they are winning. Let everyone line-up in an orderly fashion.

- Are you allowed to choose who you stand next to? If so calmly walk up to your victim. Give them a friendly smile and say something nice. Don't let them guess what you are planning.

- Wait until the queue is straight. Try to spot that look on the teacher's face that says "I've won. I have them all under control."

- Now you can give your victim that special, slightly evil grin that gives them a clue of what is about to hit them.

- Let rip – the bigger, the smellier, the noisier, the better. See how much of the line breaks up and runs for fresh air.

REPORT CARD 7

This is a real test of your powers. Can you send the line running for cover? Or will the teacher still be looking at a nicely behaved line.

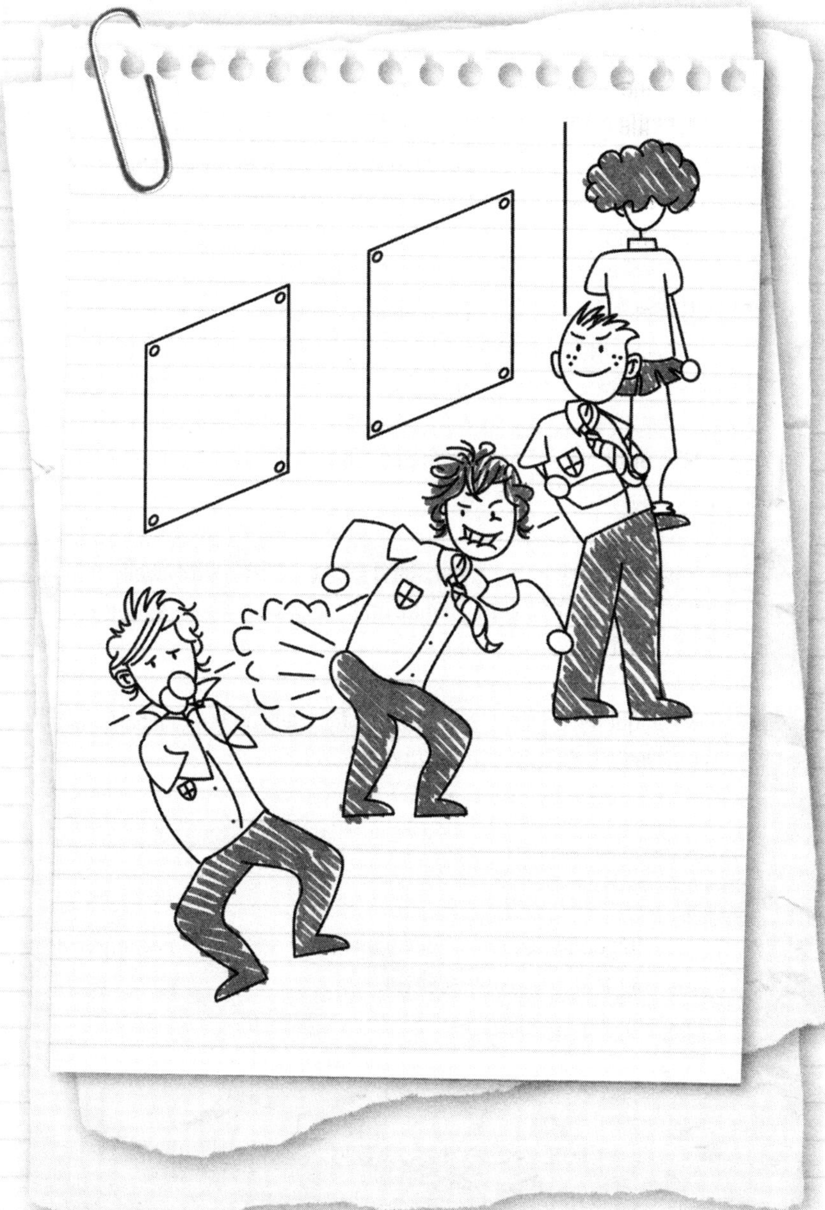

The School Play

The great farter needs an audience. Doing a buttock-blaster in front of your mates is always good fun, and shocking your victim with a silent stinker is priceless, but have you got what it takes to perform on the big stage?

- It's another Christmas play and once again you haven't been picked for the star role. Don't worry – this time you can have a tiny role and still be the centre of attention.

- Rehearsals are so dull when you have only got a couple of words to say but it is important that you pay attention this time. Think about when the best time to let rip will be. Perhaps when the angel is about to speak or just as the grand finale song has finished.

- Each time you reach that point in rehearsal play out the scene in your mind. Do an enormous 'pretend' fart and try to imagine how everyone will react.

- On the night you might be nervous but this is what helps all the great performers concentrate their powers. Wait for your moment and action! Bring the house down with one enormous bottom bugle.

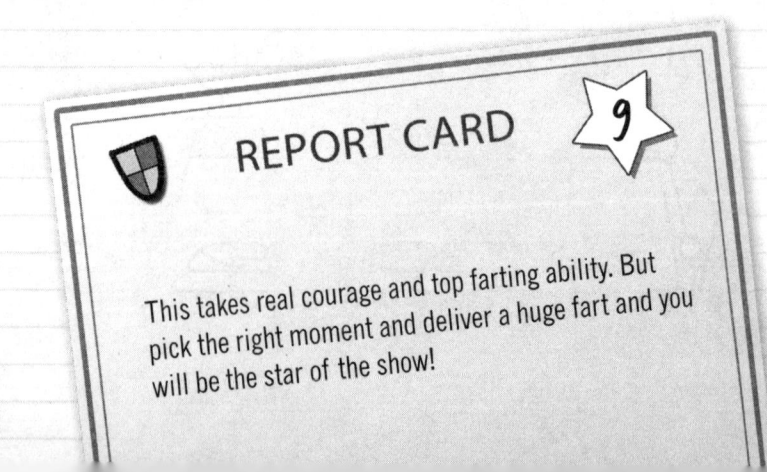

REPORT CARD — 9

This takes real courage and top farting ability. But pick the right moment and deliver a huge fart and you will be the star of the show!

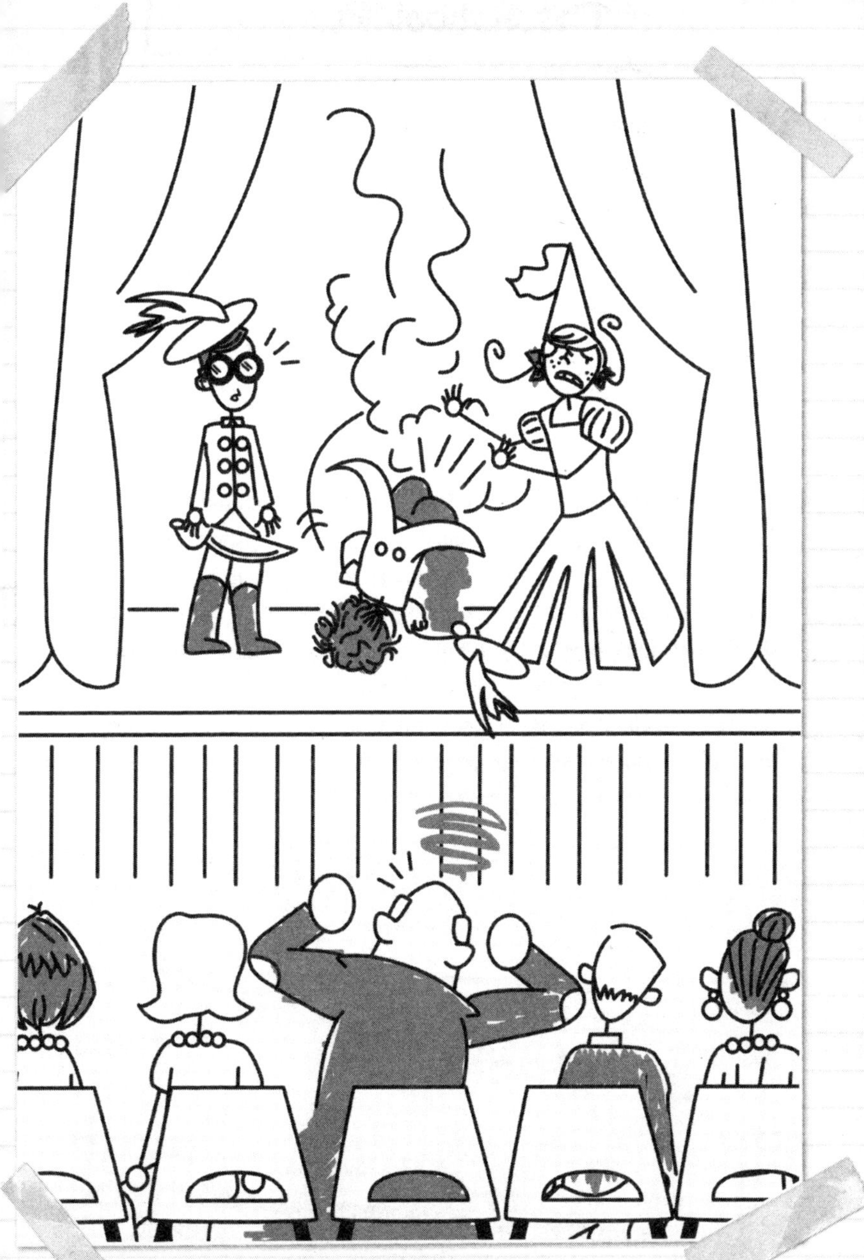

School's Out!

"Put your books away – tidily! –and form a line at the door." While some kids scramble for the exit and Little Miss Perfect folds everything up neatly and draws one more flower on her paper, you have more urgent business. To conjure up one last almighty trump that will keep you in their minds until you meet again.

- Use the scraping of chairs and the excited shouts that greet home time as a cover – there should be enough noise to cover the loudest trump you can manage.

- Don't worry that it will be wasted as all the kids disappear through the door. The teacher will be there for at least half-an-hour marking books, picking gum off the floor and wafting her book around to get rid of the smell.

- If you can't get a master blaster out in time. Save it up for when you are finally free of your teacher's gaze. Get your victim in your sights and, before they reach the school gates, say "I just wanted to say 'goodbye' – in fartese!" and let rip as loud as you can.

REPORT CARD 7

If all else fails, just let one go and stand still in the middle of the pong for a few seconds. At least it'll stop your mum giving you an embarrassing massive hug when you reach the gates.

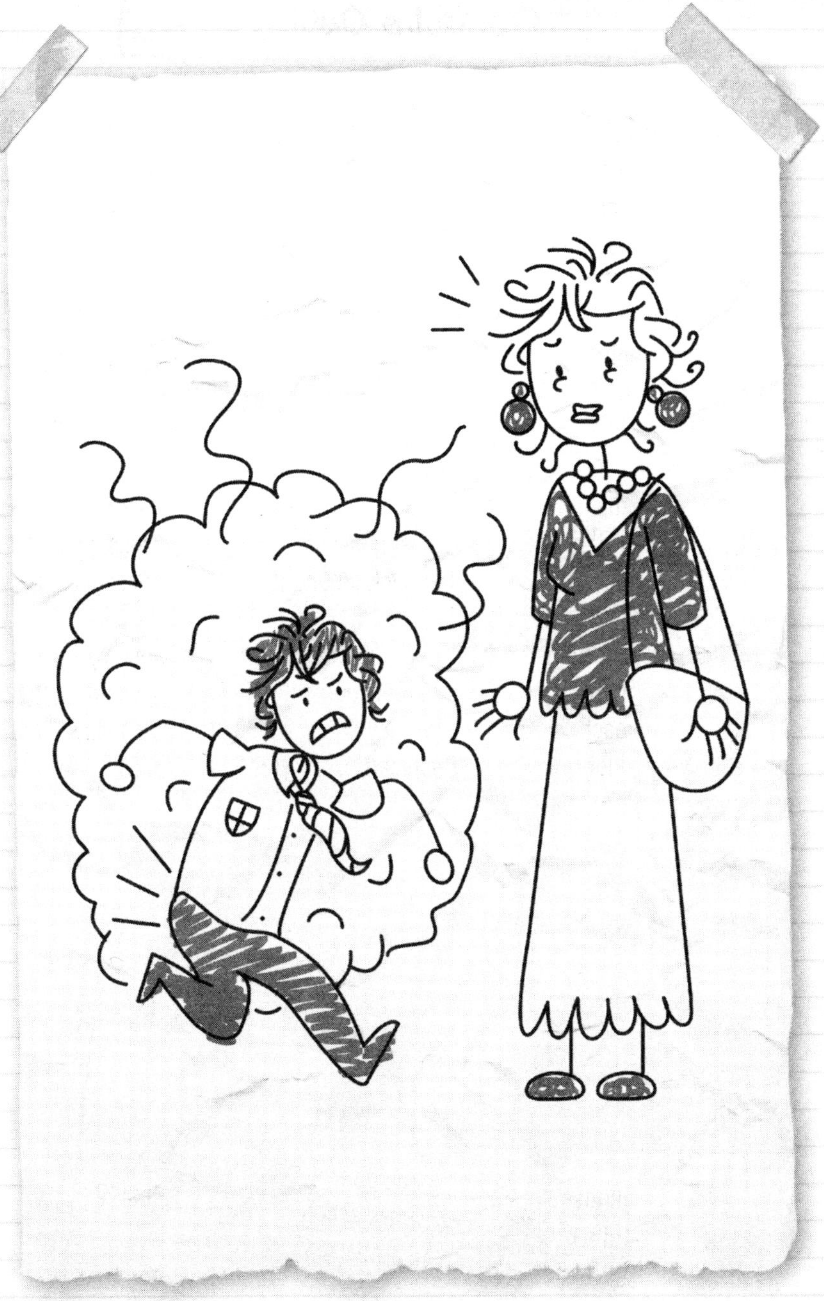

Silent But Deadly

We all like to show off, letting a real ripper explode into the air and watch everyone laugh, applaud or run away in disgust. But there are times when a little secrecy is needed, when it is important that no one knows just who the culprit is.

- To create maximum chaos. When the class is being particularly good or are all concentrating on a performance or experiment, secretly let one slip and wait for the reaction. Like counting after lightening to see how far the thunder is, count slowly (in your head!) and see how long it takes to change silence to uproar.

- To put the blame on your enemy. Be sneaky. Pick a time when they are surrounded by friends. Think of a reason to approach them – give them a fake message or tell a joke – and as you walk away drop your stinker. Retreat to a safe distance and watch the friends scatter.

- When you are on your last warning. Remember no one can prove that it was you! If the teacher has had enough of your ear-splitting trouser trumps let off some SBDs that will fill the room. He'll know it's you, the whole class will know it's you but you'll be there shrugging your shoulders – saying "What? What did I do?"

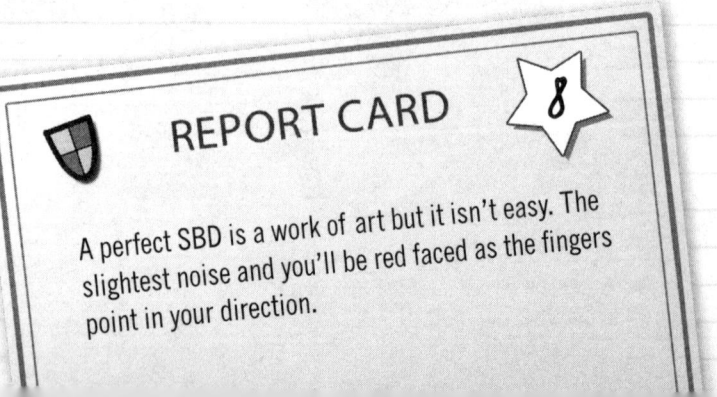

REPORT CARD

A perfect SBD is a work of art but it isn't easy. The slightest noise and you'll be red faced as the fingers point in your direction.

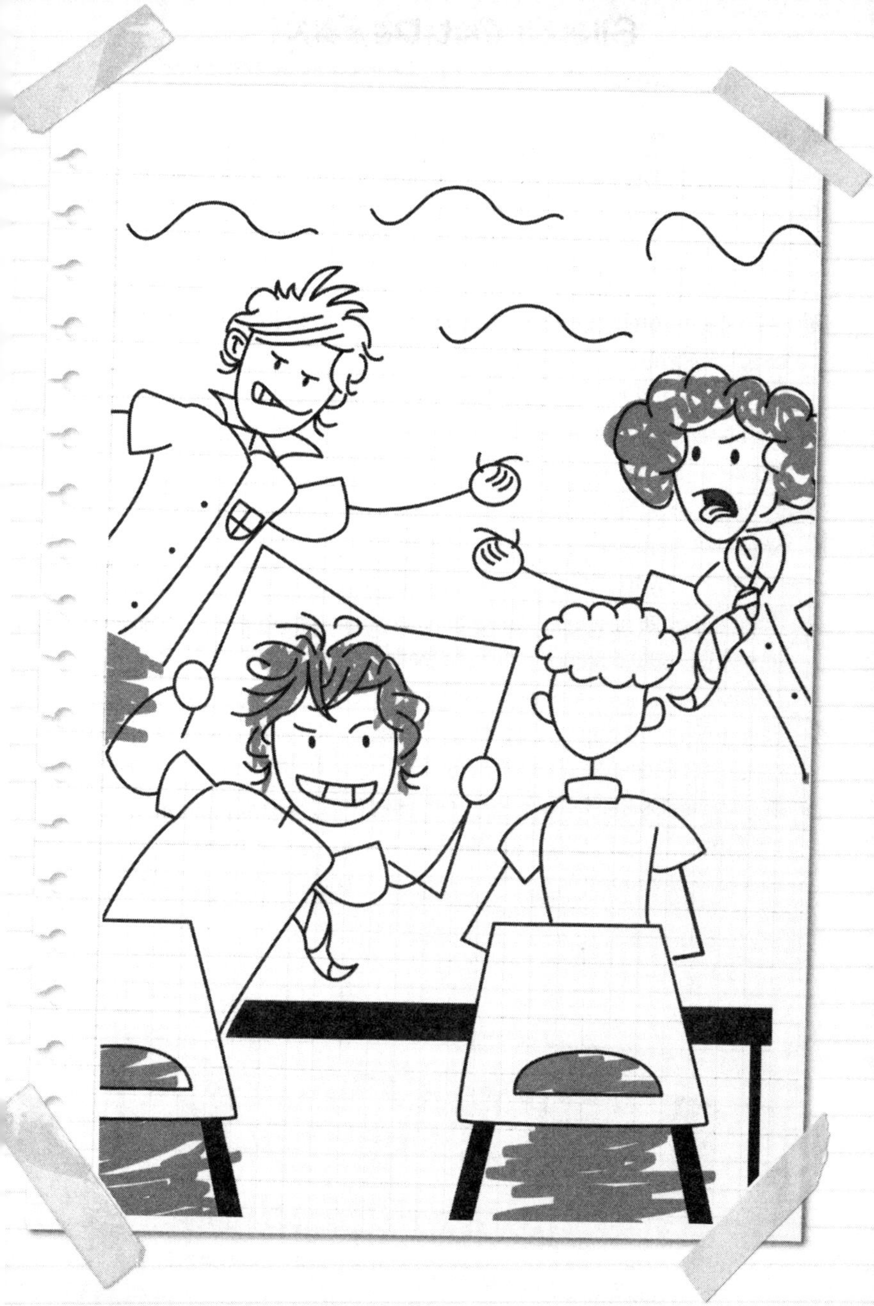

The Sporting Fart

One boy might a great shot, another have a wicked step-over, but you have the best trick of all...

All that running and stretching does something to the stomach and its contents. Let's not get too scientific here, but suffice to say it helps you brew up some choice notes from the buttock bassoon – enough to spur you to sporting success...

- It's five-all, the bell is about to end the break and Mr Popular is lining up to take a penalty. All eyes are on him and the goalkeeper – that's you! As he steps forward to take the kick, you deliver an ear-splitting cheese-cutter. Shocked, he knocks the ball wide of the posts.

- Their batsmen has been hitting the ball all over the place – it's time to sort him out. Position yourself close to the wicket and wait until he's about to hit the ball. "Owzat!" – you produce a peach of a trouser cough that's sure to get him out.

- You are neck and neck with your friend in the sports day sprint. You can see the finish line but can you get their first? Yep. You can stroll home if you let loose a bottom blast that reduces him to a helpless fit of giggles.

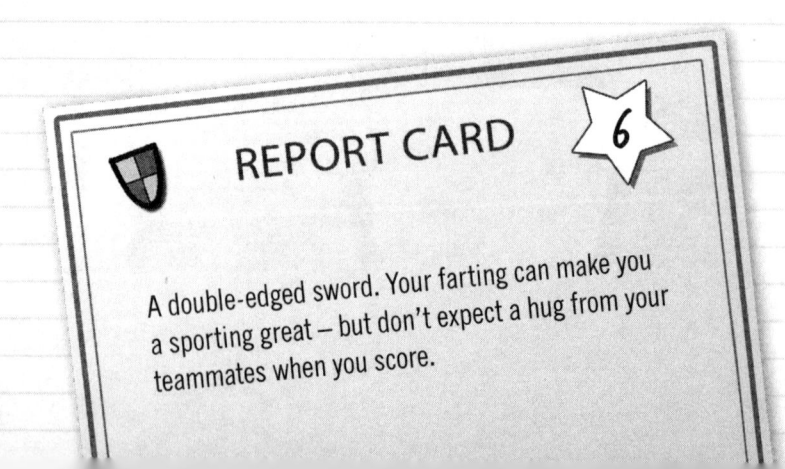

REPORT CARD 6

A double-edged sword. Your farting can make you a sporting great – but don't expect a hug from your teammates when you score.

65

Submarine

Your farts might pong a bit, but you should smell what they are like at the moment they are released from your backside. Well you shouldn't – you should get someone else to smell it. But just how do you get someone to experience the full power of your bottom bolts?

- Try laying down a real stinker in your bag and announcing loudly: "You'll never believe what I've got in here!" Encourage people to have a look. They'll find nothing but your PE kit, a homework book and a terrible smell.

- Prepare a booby trap to catch your victim. 'Accidently' drop a sweet or chocolate on the floor. Keep looking around because soon some greedy kid is bound to spot it. As he approaches, hit your bum drum. They might get their reward, but they'll pay the price – through the nose!

- Sit beside a super-tidy victim like The Swot or Little Miss Perfect. 'Accidentally' drop your pencil, calculator or book under their seat and – at the same time – drop a real belter. They'll bend down to pick up the fallen item and as they do they'll get two nostrils full of your best cheese gas!

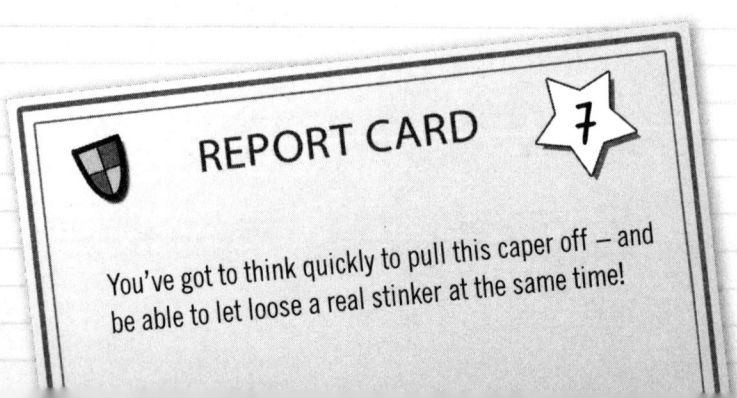

REPORT CARD ⭐ 7

You've got to think quickly to pull this caper off – and be able to let loose a real stinker at the same time!

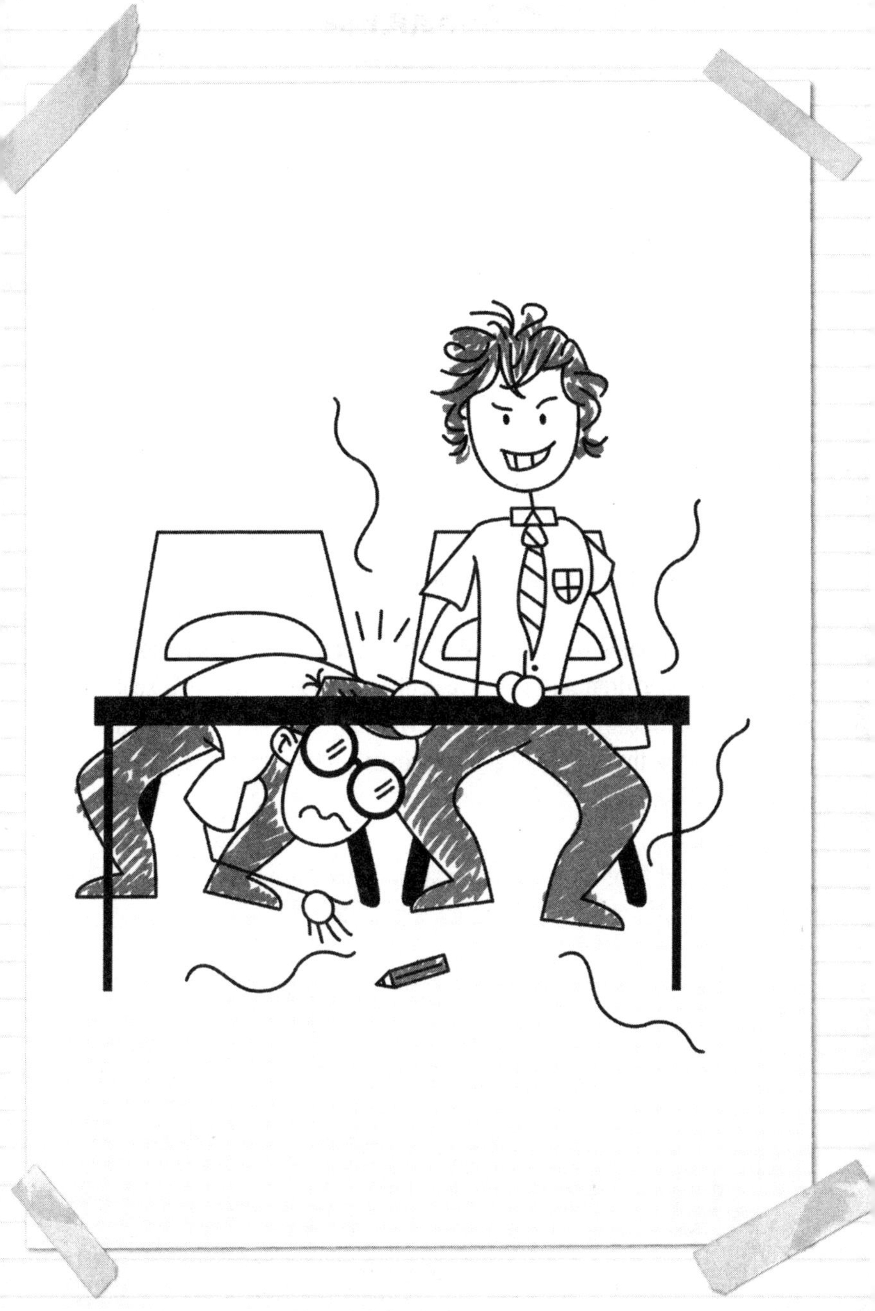

Talking Bottoms

It starts with a parp, but the battle has just begun. You need to make sure you are the winner in the battle of words that follows every trump. Do you need to put the blame for your fart on someone else? Or are you denying that it was you who cut the cheese? Or maybe, you just want to crown your superb effort with a fine choice of words.

Here are some tried and tested rhymes and lines to give you ammunition against your rivals' taunts.

Blame someone with...
- Whoever smelt it, dealt it.
- Whoever observed it, served it.
- Whoever spoke last, set off the blast.

Deny it with...
- Whoever said the rhyme did the crime.
- Whoever denied it supplied it.
- The one that sung the song made a pong.

Own it with...
- Better out than in – noisy and smelly, but it's no sin.
- Anyone seen my pet African Barking Spider?
- In with the good air out with the bad.
- There's no point in having an bottom if you don't let it sing!

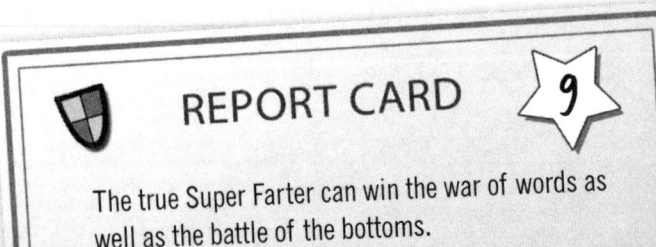

REPORT CARD 9

The true Super Farter can win the war of words as well as the battle of the bottoms.

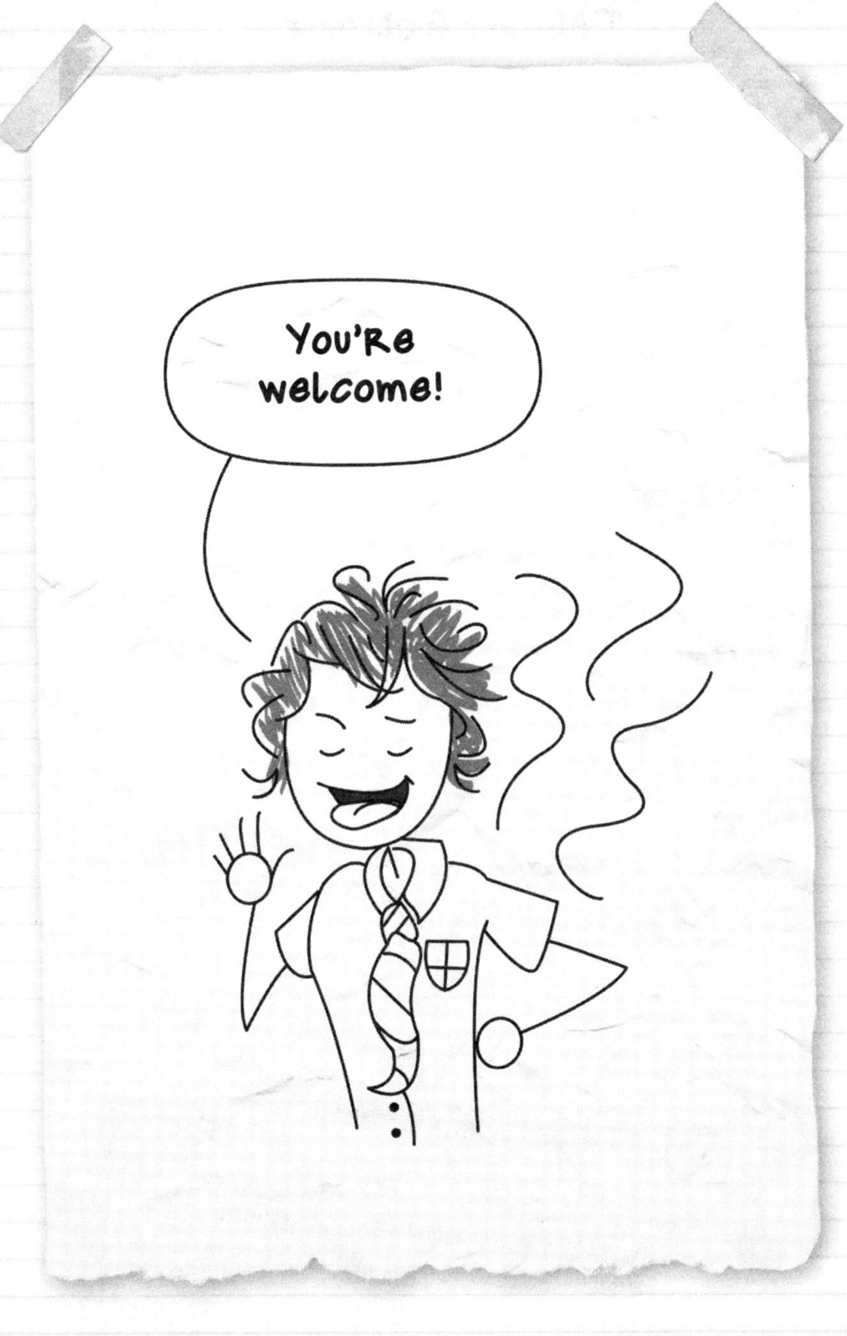
You're welcome!

The School Bus

The back seat of school buses have been specially made to make it easier to break wind and spread the fart fumes right across the bus. Ok. That's not entirely true, but it doesn't stop farting on the bus being great fun.

- Head for the back seat. It's the perfect point from which to view the effects of your efforts and it has the added advantage of being furthest from the driver so you are less likely to get caught.

- Wait until the bus has been on the road for a few minutes before blowing the bum trumpet. You need the air-conditioning to be in full flow to spread the air around the bus and make sure everyone gets the full benefit of your fart fumes.

- Once all your fellow passengers recognize you for your back-seat behaviour you can really begin to terrorize them. If there's a spare seat next to someone, go and sit next to them.

- Just watch their faces as you take your seat. All you have to do is nod and smile. They'll be thinking – "he's going to break wind any second now, I know it." After a while, just close your eyes and pretend to squeeze out a fart – now see if they look so relaxed!

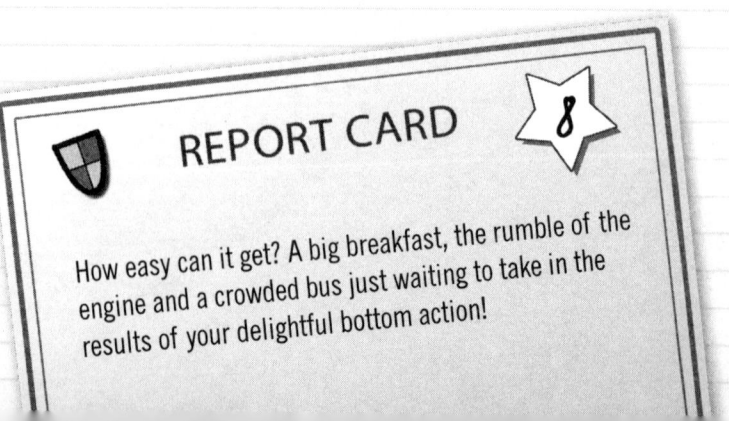

REPORT CARD

8

How easy can it get? A big breakfast, the rumble of the engine and a crowded bus just waiting to take in the results of your delightful bottom action!

71

The Swimming Pool

There's nothing like a trip to the swimming pool for getting your rear-end rifle firing. Regular gulps of air as you do your front crawl, mixed with a little pool water are the perfect ingredients for a fantastic fun fest.

- As every baby in its bathwater soon learns, even a little underwater windy-pop will produce a small bubble. A great fart-artist like you should be able to create something resembling an underwater volcano.

- See who can make the biggest bottom bubble, sneak up beside Little Miss Perfect and treat her to a personal Jacuzzi or let your friends watch as you swim off leaving a trail of bubbles.

- But beware the return to the changing room. A small area packed with others all digesting that fatal air-and-pool water brew means trouble. Have your own ammunition ready to fire or you could find yourself on the receiving end of a barrage from your rival farters.

REPORT CARD ⭐ 5

This really is too easy (with the added bonus that it's almost impossible to get caught). If you can't let one go in the pool you don't even deserve to be reading this book.

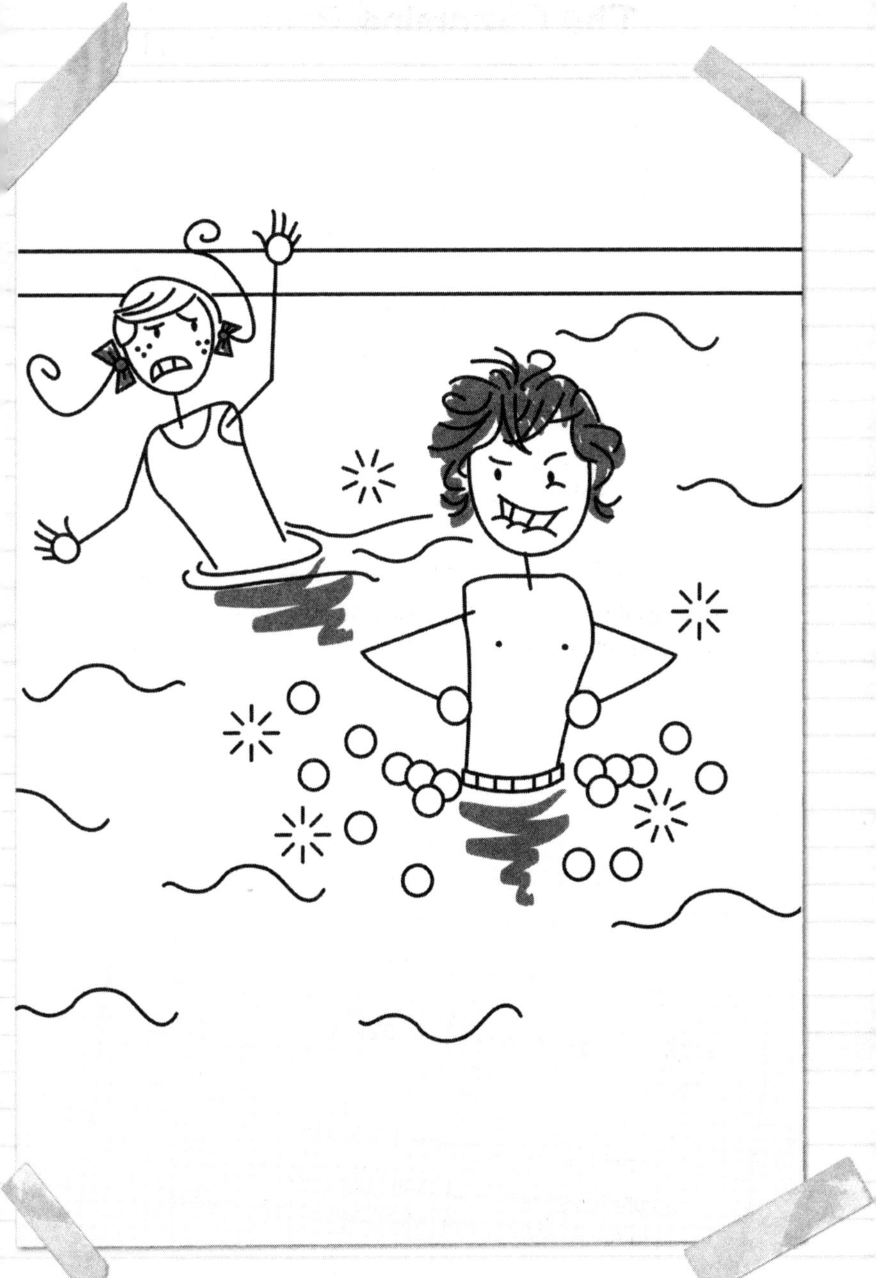

You Said "FaRt"!!

Some people don't even want to say the word let alone splat out a bad-egg belter. This is the farters' revenge – tricks to make them say the word...

- Before class begins write on the whiteboard "Hoof Hearted Ice Melted". Ask Little Miss Perfect if she knows what it means. She'll say it's nonsense, so get her to say it aloud. Then the whole class will hear her say: "Who farted? I Smelled It!"

- Tell the class you've got a great tongue-twister. One smart man, he felt smart; two smart men, they felt smart; three smart men, they felt smart! See how far they get until they say "fart".

- Write "I Shurf Artol Ot." On the whiteboard. Look at it puzzled and explain that you can't understand what it says. Wait for The Swot to look at the board and read aloud "I sure fart a lot!"

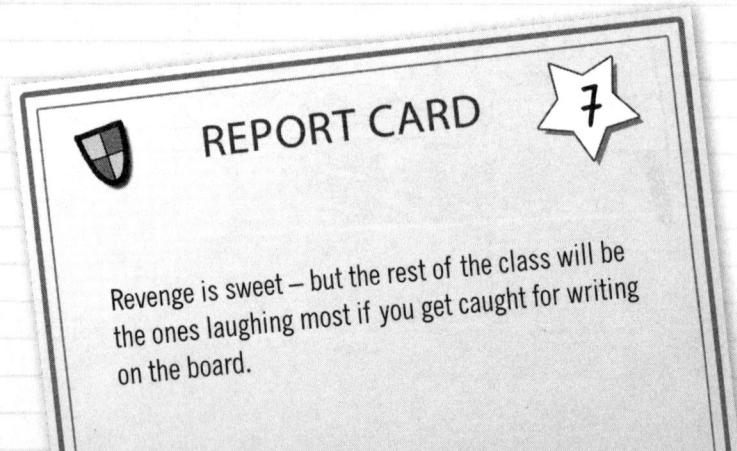

REPORT CARD 7

Revenge is sweet – but the rest of the class will be the ones laughing most if you get caught for writing on the board.

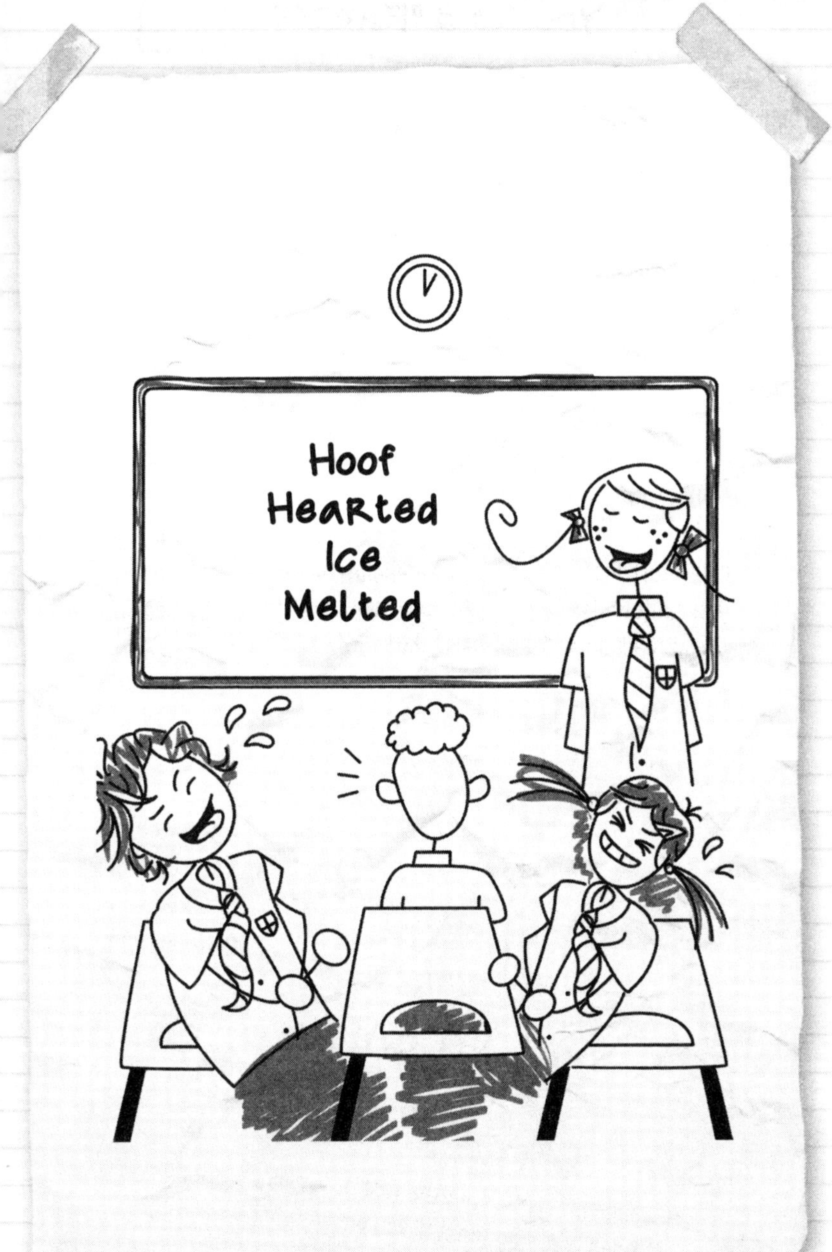
Hoof
Hearted
Ice
Melted

How Loud Can You Go?

I bet you've faced this situation... You call all your friends to hear a massive bum trumpet you have ready only to disappoint everyone by producing a tiny fart fit only for a tiny mouse. Whether you are in a farting competition or just looking to blow the ears off your friends, it's worth knowing some tricks to get your bottom blasts as loud as possible.

- Stand up and lift one leg just off the ground. Don't lift it too far though — you need to create a 'bottom funnel' to deliver the blast.

- When you feel the gas coming, hold it in for a few seconds. Let enough gas build up to deliver a strong explosion.

- Think about where you perform your pant-ripper. A room with good acoustics (where the sound echoes easily) like the bathroom, the music room or a small storeroom will make your fart sound louder than in a big hall or in the playground. Failing that, how about sticking your butt into a cupboard for extra loudness (although whoever goes next to collect the books or pencils won't be pleased!).

- Finally, if you are seated, consider what you are sitting on. A soft cushion will draw in the sound and a plastic chair will muffle the noise a little, but a hard surface will echo it back magnificently. Wooden floors are brilliant for making farts crackle, metal seats provide a crisp echo, while a stone bench will give your bottom belch a strong low tone.

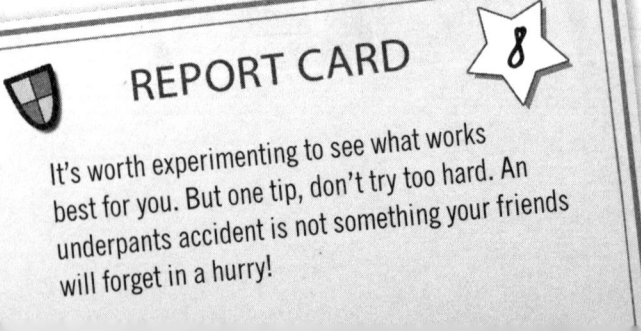

REPORT CARD

It's worth experimenting to see what works best for you. But one tip, don't try too hard. An underpants accident is not something your friends will forget in a hurry!

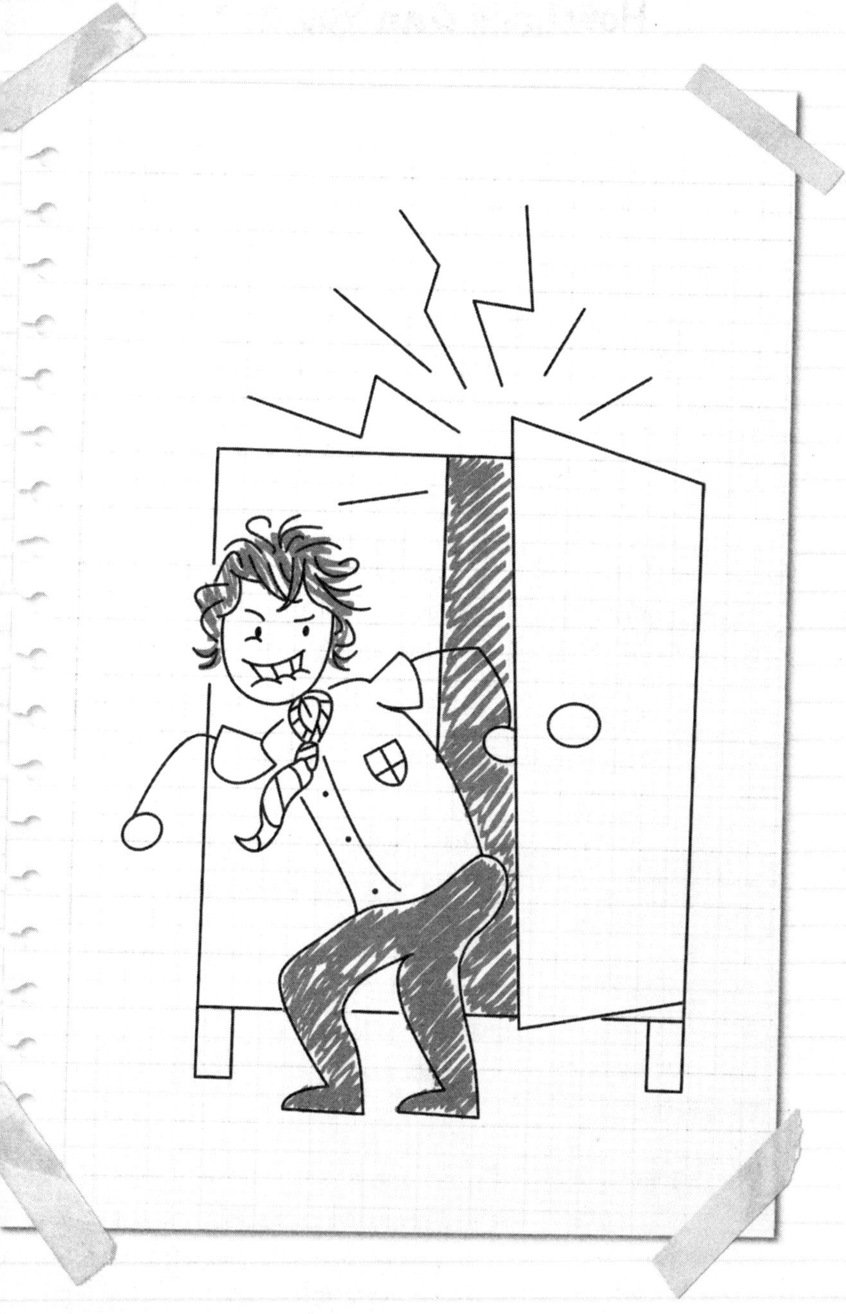

Fart Spotting

How much of a fart fanatic are you? Can you tell your 'Barn Owl' from your 'Rusty Gate'? Follow this guide and you'll be the class expert, able to identify every single one of your classmates' guffs and trumps.

The Parp
The most common fart there is. Just a single one-second sound like a quick blast on the recorder. Anyone can do one — and nearly everybody does.

The Butt-Burrrr
With this fart you still get the 'parp' but it stops suddenly and is followed by a softer and longer-lasting muffled sound. Great for getting people's attention and proving you are not just a parper.

The Barn Owl
Resembling the call of a woodland owl this is one of the funniest kinds of fart. It starts with a sound like a laugh and then turns into a drawn out yawn.

The Oops-a-Daisy
A squeaky, short pop usually let out when the farter is actually trying their best to hold it in. Often this is one perpetrated by The Swot who tries to hide it by coughing at the same time.

The Chinese Firecracker
Anything from four to 20 (the more the better) quick-fire farts that get louder and louder. Will quickly draw a crowd who will wonder just when it is going to end.

The Dribbler
The opposite of the Firecracker. Though equal in number, these farts get gradually softer and quieter until they disappear completely much to the disappointment of those who come to watch.

The Medicine Ball
Drops like a heavy weight as if the lower half of your tummy has given way. The brief but loud 'Thud!' is often followed by a real meaty whiff of rotting bananas and old socks.

The Ripper
This is the big one! A honking blast that can be heard in the next town. It's a clear-the-room fart that will make you a hero for at least the rest of the afternoon.

The Rusty Gate
A drawn out squeak that lasts for two or three seconds. This usually carries a fearsome whiff that is best avoided.

The Shot Gun
Like a backfiring car or a firework-night banger this fart is sudden, explosive and over almost as soon as it has begun. Stand clear though — there's often another being loaded a minute or so later.

The Muffler
Was that a fart? Or did someone sit down quickly and produce a whoosh of air from the chair. It won't be long before you discover the truth, as this puff of a fart produces a cheesy-mustard stench that makes it hard to remain in the same postcode.

Do the Splits

Ripppppp! We all live in dread of that terrible sound. Splitting your trousers is one of the most embarrassing things that can happen to you in the school day. But when it happens to someone else – well, that's a different matter, it's hilarious. And if it doesn't happen to them, you can always pretend it has and watch their reaction.

- Bring to school a piece of old clothing that you no longer need.

- Place a coin on the floor and position yourself nearby, but out of sight.

- Begin a tear in your piece of cloth and wait for your victim to approach.

- He should notice the coin and start to bend down to pick it up.

- At the very moment that he bends down to pick up the coin, rip the cloth as loudly as possible.

- Enjoy the fun as they reach behind to see if they ripped their trousers and see just how red their faces have gone.

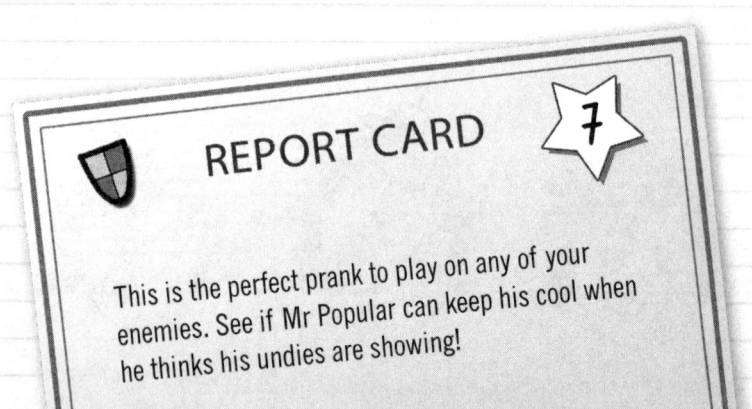

REPORT CARD

7

This is the perfect prank to play on any of your enemies. See if Mr Popular can keep his cool when he thinks his undies are showing!

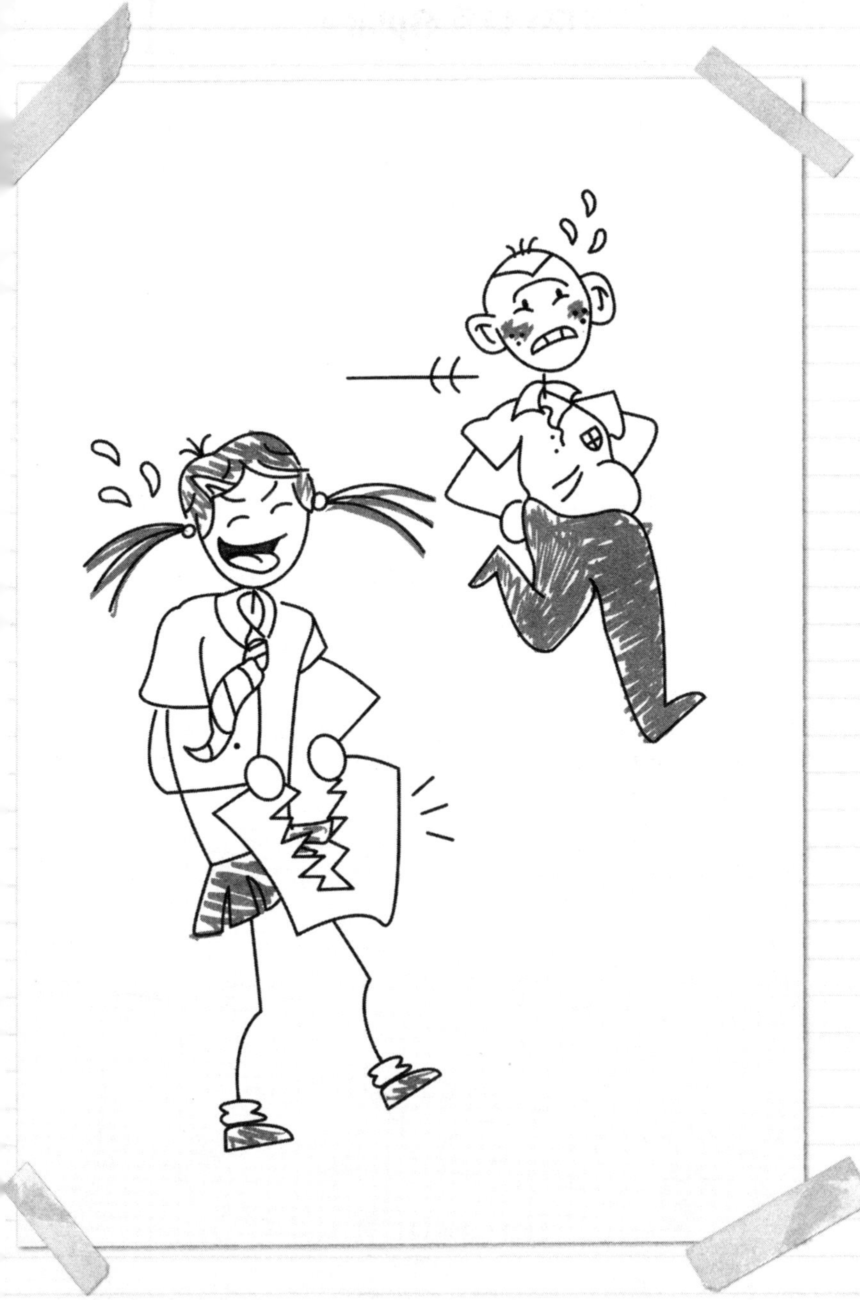

What Time is it?

Doesn't time fly when you are having fun? But it can go so much faster when some prankster starts playing with the class clock. A little turn of the big hand and you'll have confused teachers, extended breaks and school ending early.

- Try to find yourself in a seat nearest the classroom clock. Otherwise you'll have to persuade the person sitting nearest to do this.

- When the teacher leaves the room, stand on your chair and take the clock off the wall.

- Look on the back. There should be a knob you can twist that turns the minute hand of the clock.

- Move the hand so the clock is 15 minutes ahead of the real time. That should be a small enough amount to stop him noticing.

- If you get another chance you can do it again (and again) but only in 15 minute chunks.

If your teacher is up for some fun you can prank a classmate with this trick. Next time one of the class falls asleep, the whole class should creep out of the room into the corridor. The teacher should set the clock to five o'clock and leave too. He can immediately return and wake the pupil – saying everyone has gone home. He'll grab his things and rush out – only to find his class laughing in the corridor!

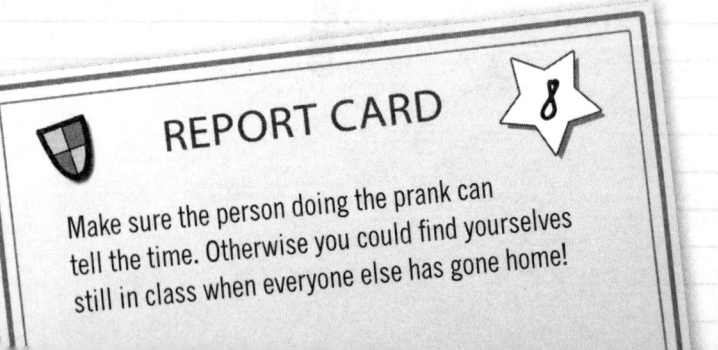

REPORT CARD

Make sure the person doing the prank can tell the time. Otherwise you could find yourselves still in class when everyone else has gone home!

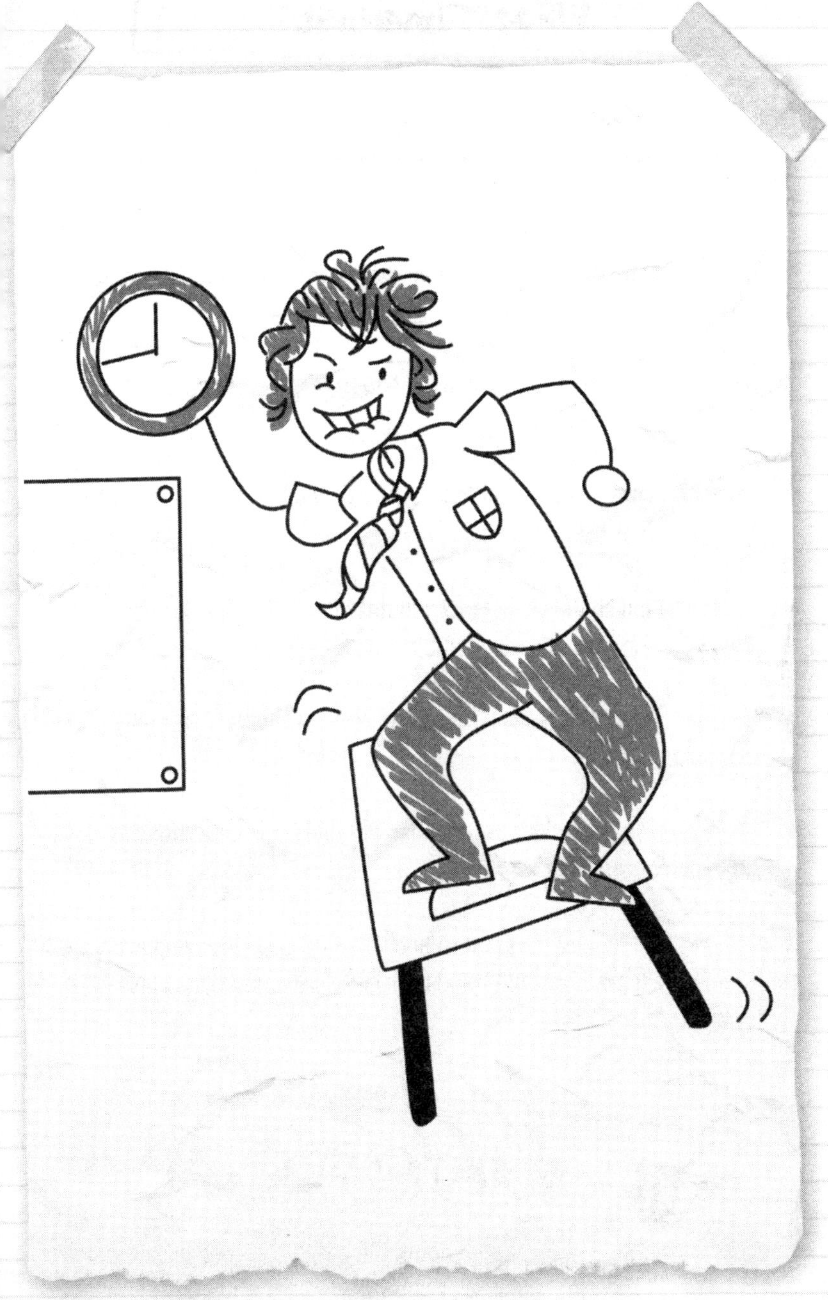

Door Ambush

This is the most classic and simple prank ever which leaves one poor soul soaked and the rest of the class helpless with laughter. An object is balanced on the top of the classroom door, someone enters and the rest is gravity...

- Fill a bucket (a plastic one, we don't want anyone going to hospital!) with water.

- Stand on a chair that is high enough so you can reach the top of the classroom door.

- Close the door enough to be able to balance the bucket on the top and lean the side on the wall above the door.

- Climb down, take the chair away and retreat a safe distance.

Now for the fun bit... Who'll be the first through the door? It could be your teacher, but what if it's the Head, a visiting VIP or even the Prime Minister? It's too late to back down now – cross your fingers and wait...

- Whoever pushes the door even a little will find the bucket crashing down and receive a right royal soaking!

- If you're feeling a little too nervous about a big bucket of water, you could try a paper plate piled high with ripped up pieces of paper, a shoe or a football!

REPORT CARD — 5

Why only five out of ten? Whether you succeed or get caught in the act, you are sure to get found out. Just don't tell them you got the idea from this book, ok?

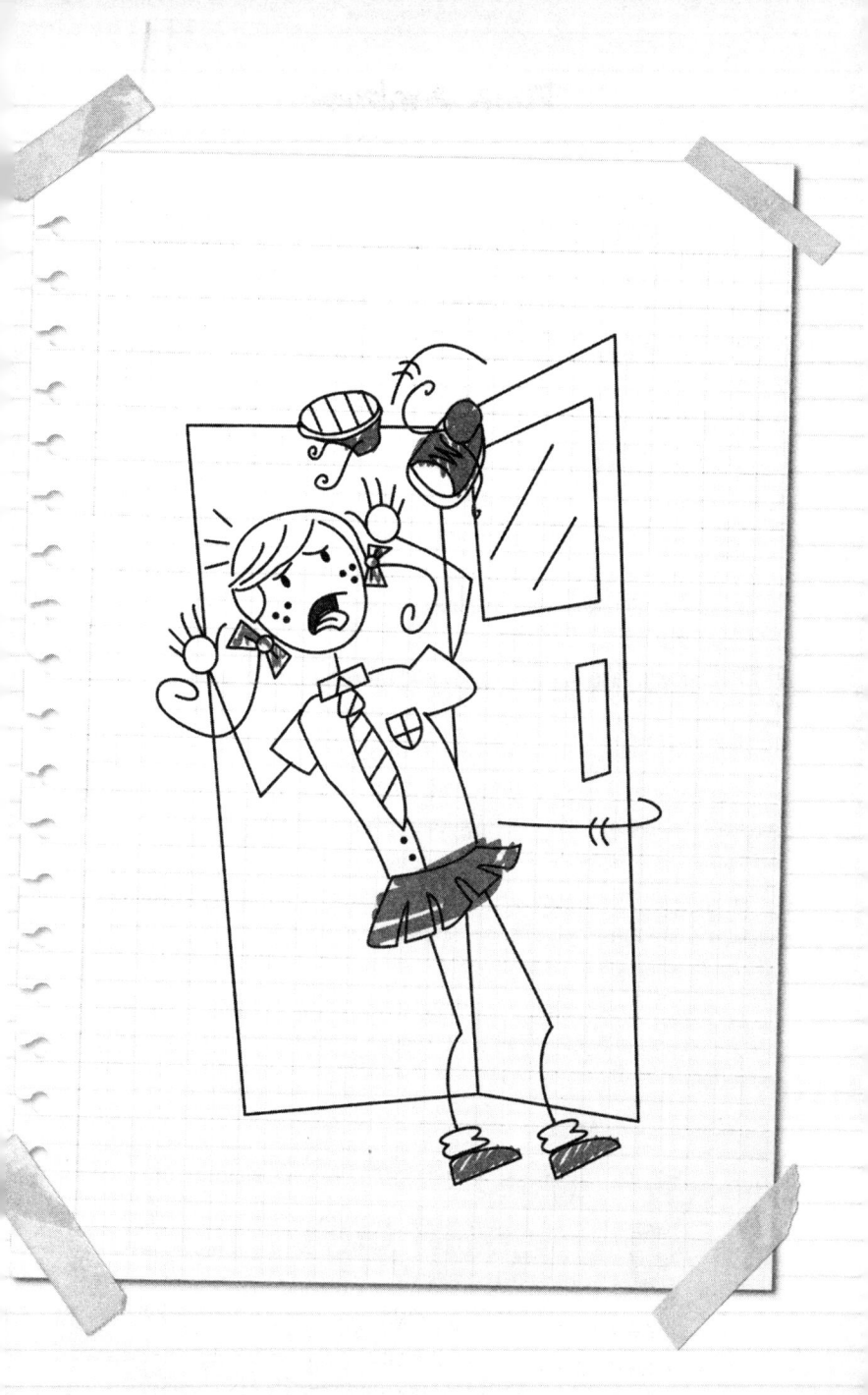

Empty Room

"Ok Class. I've written some adjectives on the whiteboard. Who can tell me what... what? Class? Where have my class gone?"

Can a teacher lose her whole class? In the middle of a lesson? If you pull this prank off successfully, she might just think she has.

- Pick a time when you are all sitting at your desks or tables.

- Wait until the teacher's focus is elsewhere. If she's pinning something to a wall or trying to get the computer to work.

- Silently point to the ground. Making sure the whole class sees you.

- As quietly as possible everyone must slide down beneath the tables.

- When your teacher looks up, all she will see is rows of empty desks.

Imagine what it will look like. One moment she is teaching a full class, the next there is no one there at all. Of course, she is going to realize what has happened pretty quickly but you'll be fine if you have your excuses worked out in advance, something like "I was just picking my pencil up" or "my shoelaces had come undone."

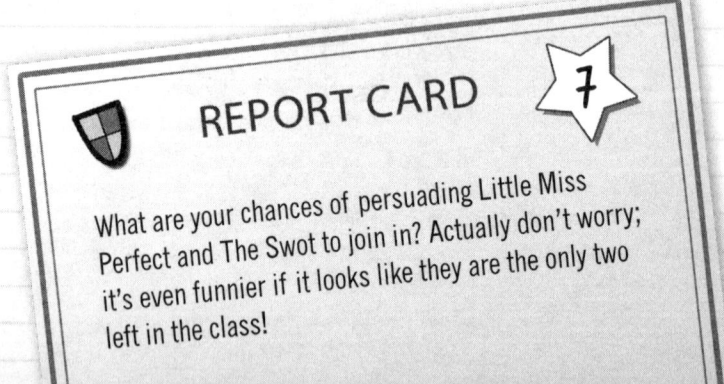

REPORT CARD 7

What are your chances of persuading Little Miss Perfect and The Swot to join in? Actually don't worry; it's even funnier if it looks like they are the only two left in the class!

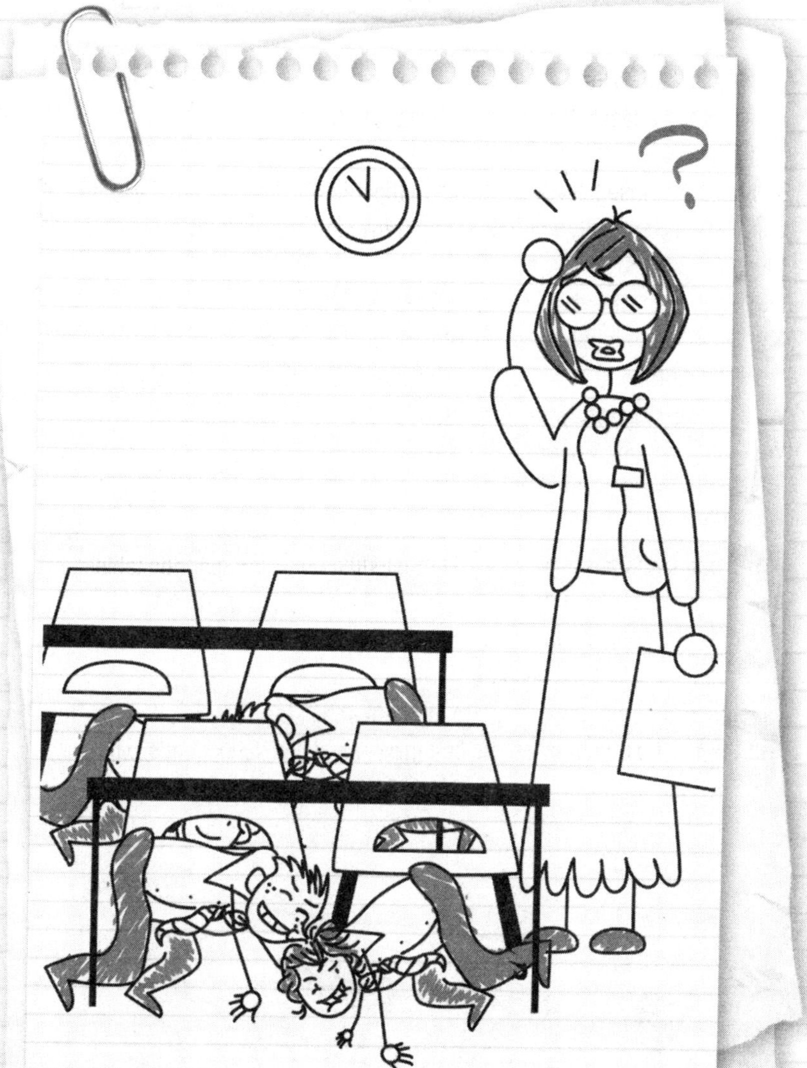

Hide and Don't Seek

"Ready or not – I'm not coming."

Really funny for you – but you'll be the only one laughing and the rest of the class probably won't talk to you for a week – even your friends. Still, that'll serve them right for wanting the play the dullest playground game ever invented (next to skipping).

You know that feeling when you are hiding in a game of hide and seek and you start to feel that no one is actually seeking? Do you give up and come out of your hiding place or do you stay hidden (after all it is a great hiding place)? Well in this prank, you are the seeker – who doesn't seek. Just to see how long it will take them to emerge.

Make sure everyone is playing – your friends, rivals and enemies. You can only play this once – play along with them for a while. "I'm terrible at this – it will take me ages to find you." Read a book. How long will the hiders wait before they realize you are not seeking?

Will they still be there when the bell goes – or when school ends?

REPORT CARD

Make sure you never have to be the seeker again

Hands Full

Who's the most competitive in the class? You know, the one who always thinks they can do everything best and who can't bear to lose at anything? They are about to become the perfect victim of a great prank.

- You'll need two paper cups three-quarters full of water.

- Approach your victim and say, "Look at this brilliant trick!"

- Then put your hand palm-down on the table and balance one of the cups of water on the back of your hand.

- They won't be too impressed. Agree and say it would be so much better if you could balance a cup on both hands.

- If you've picked the right victim they are sure to claim that they could balance both cups. You should look doubtful, but tell them to go ahead and that you'll even help them get them on.

- Sit them down with both palms down. Balance one cup of water on one hand and one on the other.

- Say "Wow, that's great but I've got to rush" and then hurry away.

- They'll be trapped, unable to move without spilling the water all down them!

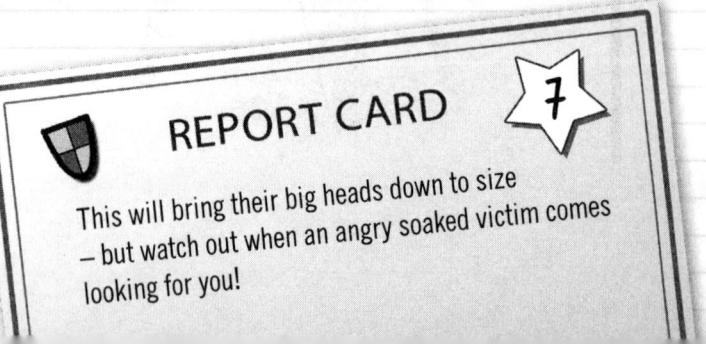

REPORT CARD — 7

This will bring their big heads down to size — but watch out when an angry soaked victim comes looking for you!

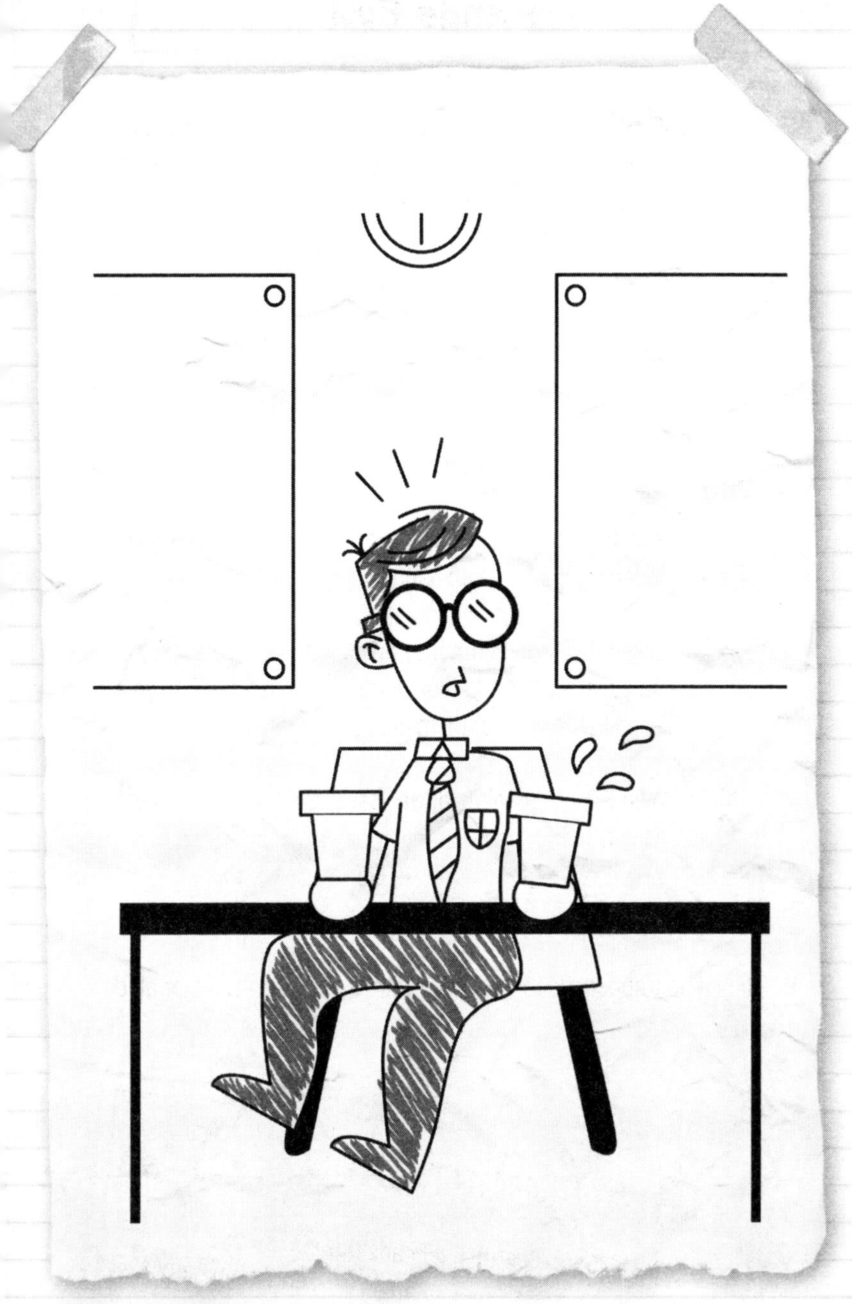

I ♥ Teacher

"Give it to me!" Your teacher holds his hand out angrily "Now let's see what's more interesting than what I've got to say." Reluctantly you hand over the scrap of paper you were about to pass to your friend. He unfolds it and reads it aloud to the class. "I just did an awesome fart wait until Big Nose smells it."

It's embarrassing and humiliating. But there is a way of getting him back. Next time, prepare your note in advance. Now comes the difficult part. Pass your note so that he's bound to see you – but make it look like you don't want to be caught. He'll grab the note but this time it will say something like…

"What a fascinating lesson! He's a brilliant teacher."

Or…

"My mum thinks he's is really cute."

Or even…

"I love maths… I'm going to do more sums when I get home."

Now watch his face and see how red he can get!

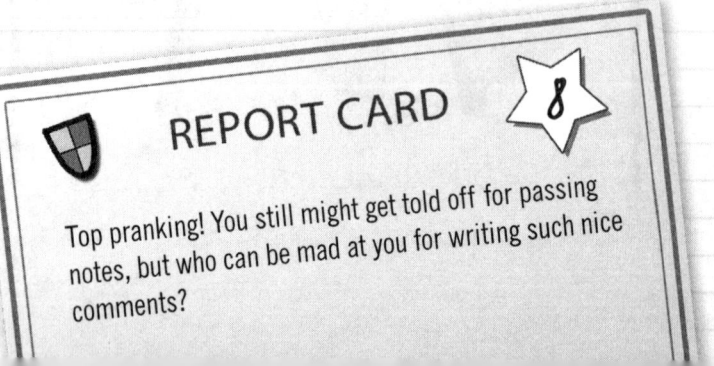

REPORT CARD

Top pranking! You still might get told off for passing notes, but who can be mad at you for writing such nice comments?

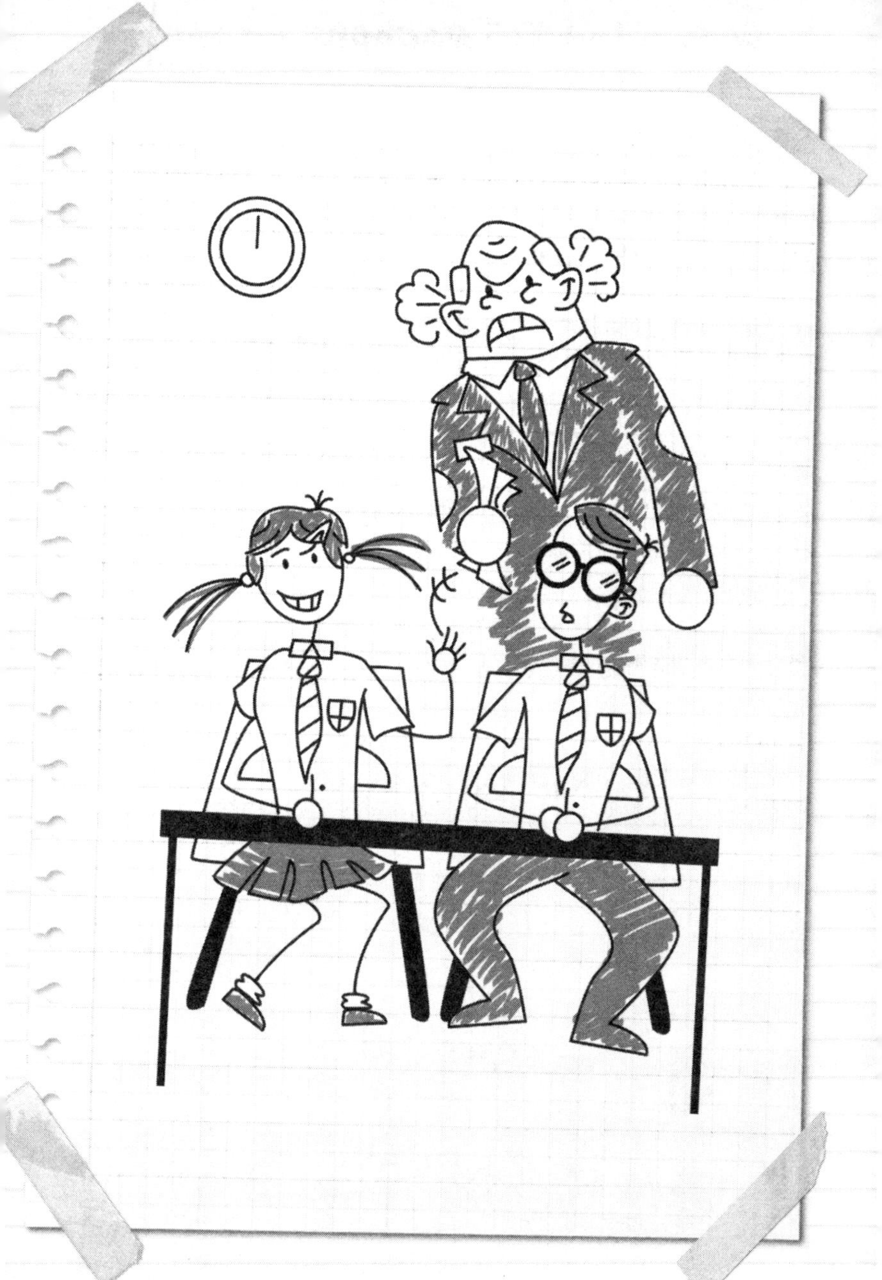

Lost in the Toilet Paper Factory

Everybody has to make the trip to the boys' or the girls' loos sooner or later. There's no use trying to hold it in! It's a private time, when we just want to get in and out as soon as possible. What you don't want is a message from the outside world. But that's just what the class prankster has arranged…

- Taking a pen with you, sneak into the toilet when no one is watching.

- Lock the cubicle door while you arrange the prank.

- Unravel the toilet roll until you are 30 or so squares along the roll.

- Disguising your handwriting, write on the next piece of paper: "Help! I'm trapped in a toilet paper factory."

- Carefully roll the paper back, so it looks exactly as it did when you started.

- Leave as if nothing has happened and wait until a few people use the toilet. Pretty soon someone will be in for a big shock!

REPORT CARD 2

This can be a real non-event if the finder just ignores the message. But if you are lucky, it's amazing when the victim decides to show the message to the teacher!

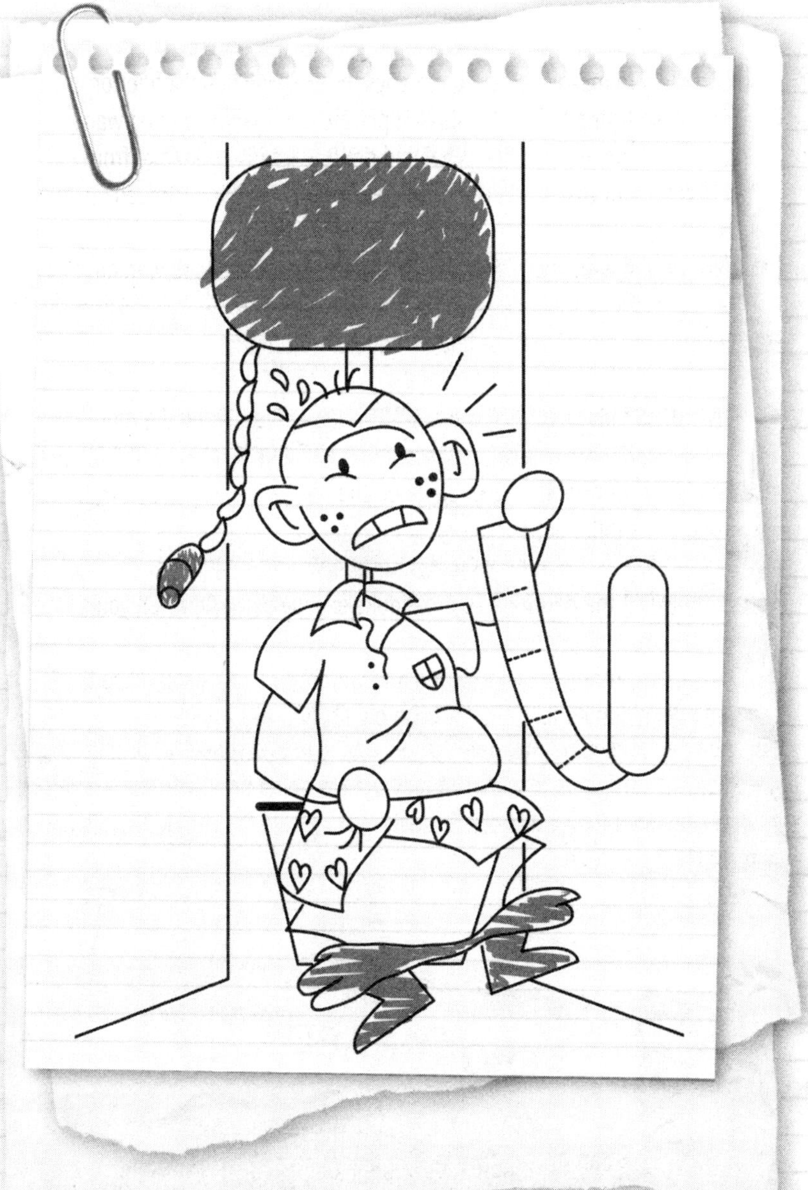

The Magic Spot

Would you like to really stun your teacher? Get the whole class to pretend there's a spot on the floor that makes them all sit up and pay attention. This prank involves the whole class working together, so you'll have to work hard to rope in the goody-goodies, wimpy kids and those who think they're too cool.

- When your teacher leaves the room, explain to the class that you are all going to pretend there is a spot in the room where the teacher will suddenly get everyone's attention.

- When she passes over or stands at that spot everyone must suddenly sit up straight and focus on the teacher – when she moves away everyone should relax and slouch again.

- If it works well, try it out with other prompts – when the teacher says a certain word, when a particular classmate answers a question or gets told off...

The sight of all the kids sitting up together without any apparent command will leave the teacher completely baffled and give everyone else a right giggle. Watch as she struggles to work out just what is going on – with the whole class in on the joke. As long as no one squeals and reveals the prank, there's hours of fun to be had!

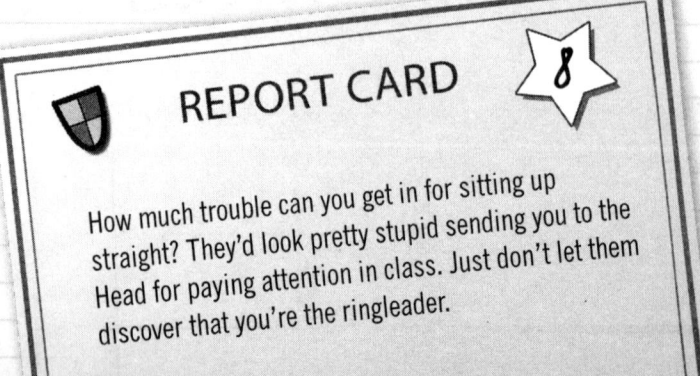

REPORT CARD

How much trouble can you get in for sitting up straight? They'd look pretty stupid sending you to the Head for paying attention in class. Just don't let them discover that you're the ringleader.

97

On the Money

This is a nice and simple trick – which doesn't work. Confused? Ok, I'll go slowly. You are going to ask your friend if he wants to help in a disappearing coin trick. However, the real trick is that the coin won't disappear but he ends up looking a little foolish.

- Tell your friend that for the trick to work he needs to do exactly as you ask.

- Place a large round coin (a 10p or 2p piece) on a piece of paper.

- Get the friend to hold it in place with one finger and draw round it with a thick pencil (or a felt tip pen if you are feeling mean).

- Pause for a second and ask them to try another finger – just in case. And a third one for good luck.

- Then get your friend (or should I say victim) to pick up the coin and roll it along the bridge of their nose.

- Take the coin off them and look at it in disbelief, amazed it is still there.

- Now turn away, as if you are disappointed but really so they don't see you laughing at the black line they've drawn along their nose.

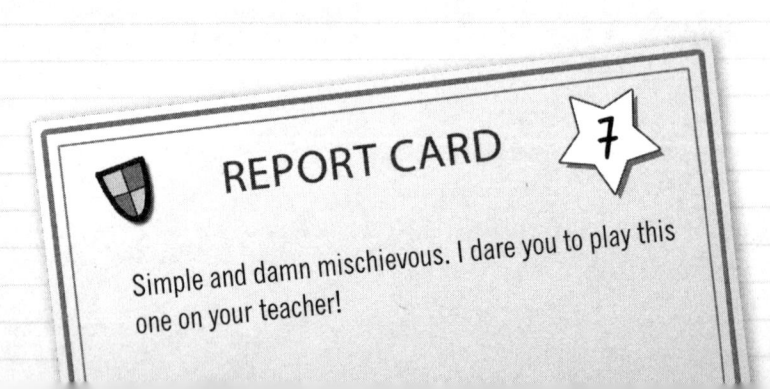

REPORT CARD 7

Simple and damn mischievous. I dare you to play this one on your teacher!

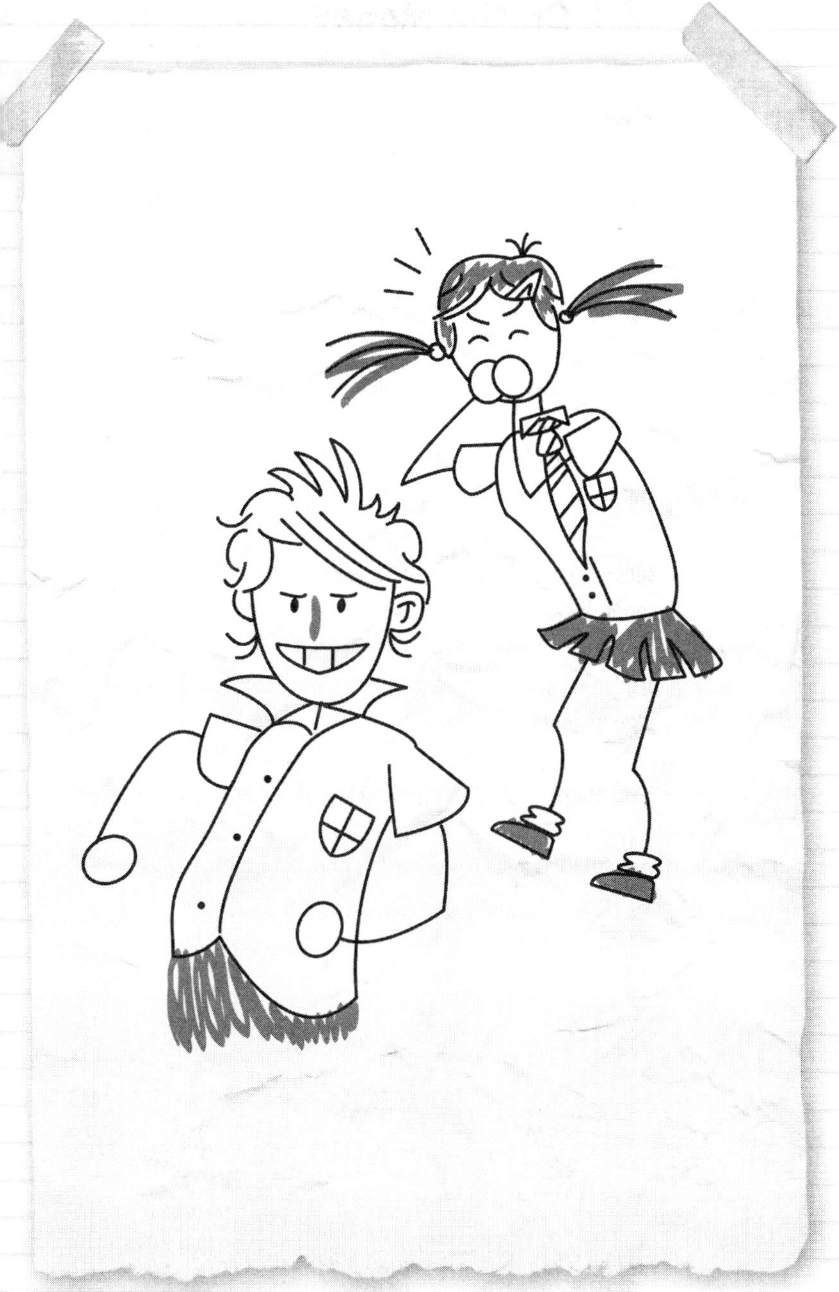

Packed-Back Backpack

There are certain things all kids should know before they leave junior school. Things like how to do their times tables, how to use an adjective, how to say "Hello" in French — and how to 'Nugget' a backpack. The first three are down to the school, but here's how to learn the essential skill of 'nuggeting'...

- Without them noticing 'borrow' your victim's backpack.

- Remove all the contents from the backpack's main compartment.

- Carefully pull the backpack from the inside so that it turns inside out.

- Put all the contents back into the bag along with a note saying "Congratulations! You've Been Nugetted!"

- Zip up the bag, making sure that the shoulder straps are tucked inside.

- Return the bag to exactly the same place that you found it.

Sounds simple, but when they go to find their bag your victim will be confused. They'll find their backpack looks more like a chicken nugget, has no straps to put their arms through and will have to work hard to find exactly where the zip has got to!

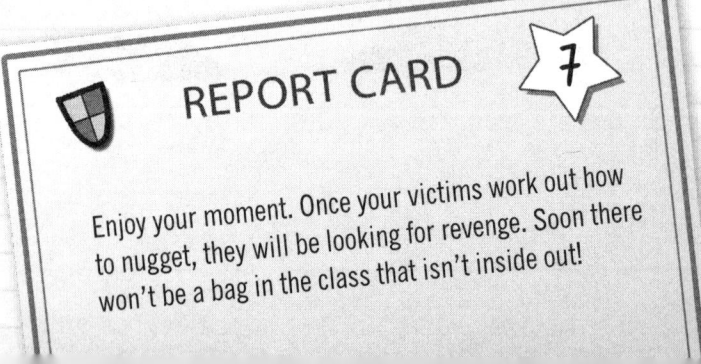

REPORT CARD 7

Enjoy your moment. Once your victims work out how to nugget, they will be looking for revenge. Soon there won't be a bag in the class that isn't inside out!

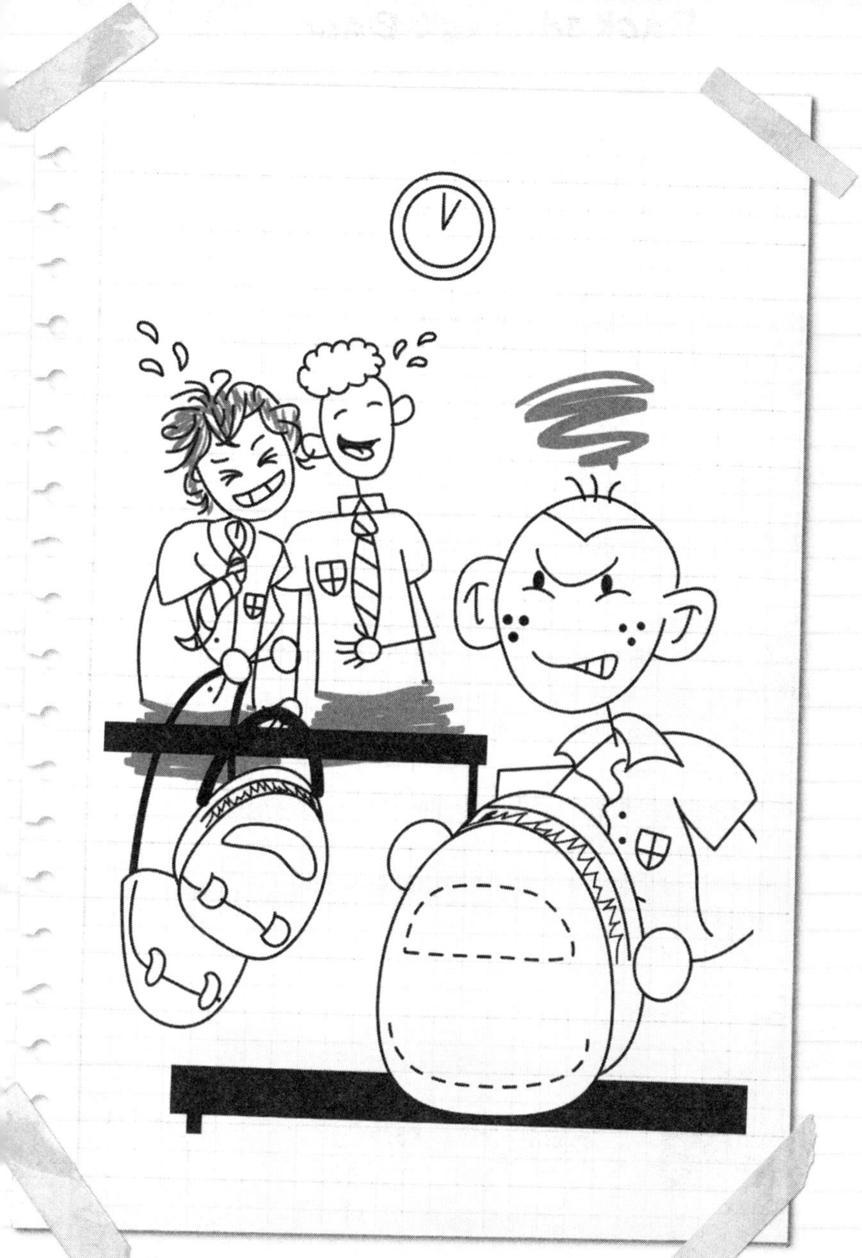

Pin the Glass

Hey you big boaster! Fancy going round saying you know how to pin a glass of water to the wall. Now everyone will be insisting you show them how you do it. Brilliant! Now just pick which of your doubters would look best with their hair dripping wet.

- Get a glass of water – a real glass or a cup, not a paper cup – and a pin.

- Make a big show of finding the right place for your performance.

- Hold the glass up to the wall about head height.

- Start trying to push the pin through the glass.

- 'Accidentally' drop the pin on the floor by your feet.

- Tell your audience that you've managed to get the glass exactly in position but you need the pin.

- Pick your victim and politely ask them to get the pin for you.

- As they bend down to pick it up, pour the water from the glass right on their head.

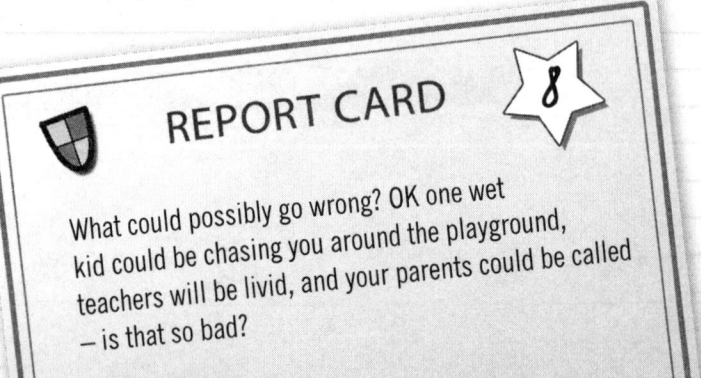

REPORT CARD

What could possibly go wrong? OK one wet kid could be chasing you around the playground, teachers will be livid, and your parents could be called – is that so bad?

103

A Curious Class

We've given the teacher such a hard time; maybe it's time to ease up on her a little. This little bit of fun just requires you to be interested in what she is saying. Like, really interested. Really, really interested. Because you are going to ask a question, and another and another until, guess what? You've driven her to distraction – again!

- Pick a lesson you are not keen on. One of those afternoon ones when you really want to be having much more fun.

- Let the teacher begin the class. After a minute someone should ask a question – as intelligent a question as possible.

- As your teacher begins to answer, ask her more and more questions.

- If you get stuck, try thinking of the six W's – What? Where? Why? Which? When? Who?

- When it seems like she has finally explained, shake your head in a puzzled way and say "I still don't get it."

- Have a rest for a minute or to and then return to the questioning – ask about things she was talking about five minutes ago or even yesterday in a different subject, ask the meaning of every word right down to the smallest – "what does 'and' mean exactly?"

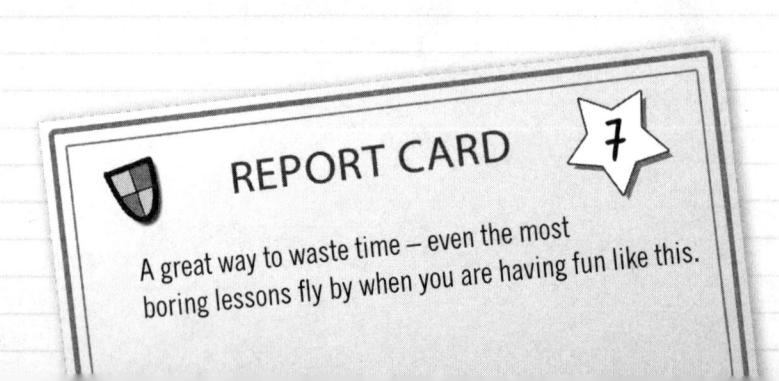

REPORT CARD ⭐ 7

A great way to waste time – even the most boring lessons fly by when you are having fun like this.

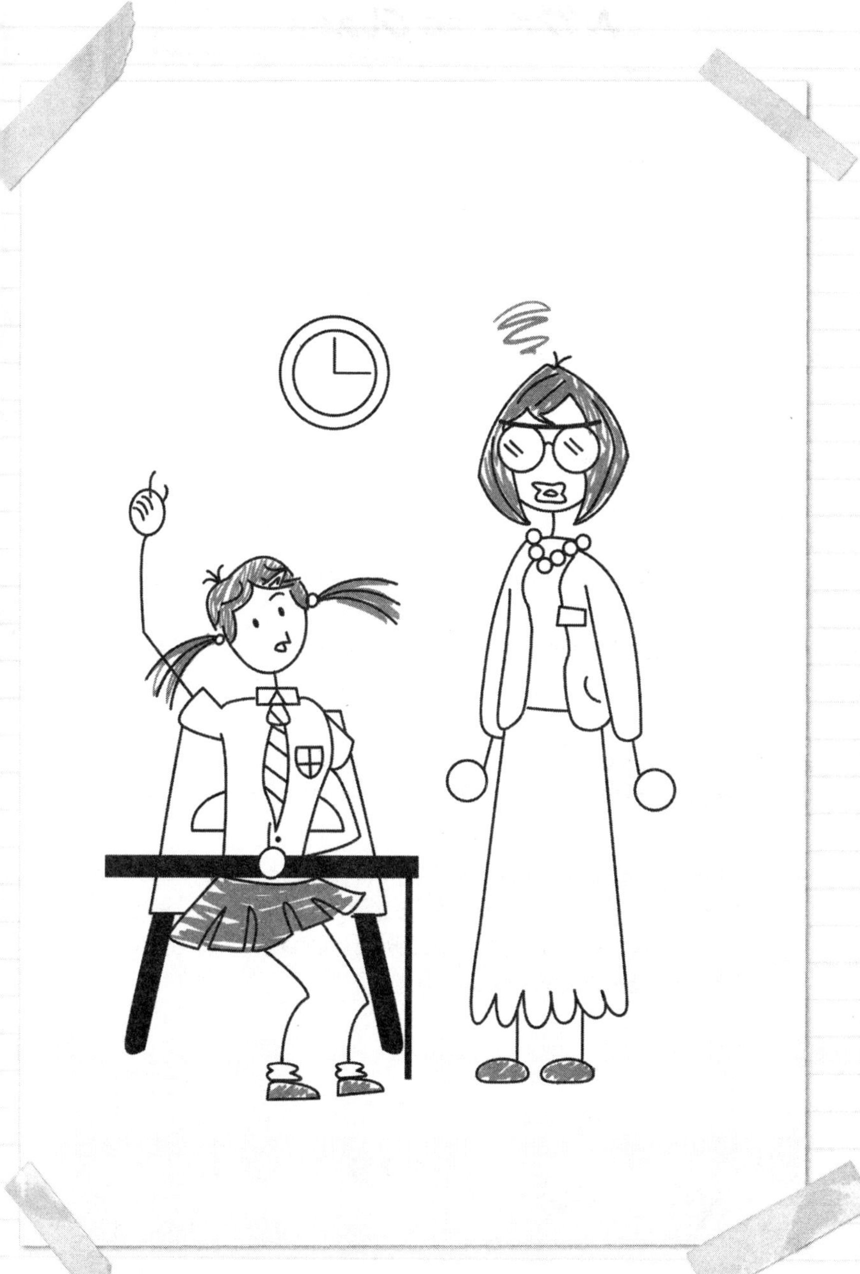

Sticky Note Car

It's been a long wait but at last the summer holidays have arrived. Maybe you'll be back in six weeks or time or perhaps you're all moving on to secondary school. Either way there's still time for one last prank to make sure you are not forgotten – so best make it a good 'un.

- You and your handpicked team are going to completely cover your teacher's car in sticky notes (the small squares of paper – usually yellow, green or pink – with a sticky stripe at the top).

- You'll need a look-out and several hard-pranking friends to help you.

- Buy as many packets of sticky notes – of different colours – as you can with your pocket money. Tell your parents it is for a school project – you won't be lying really!

- Work out just which car is your teacher's – you don't want to waste time (and stationary) on the wrong one.

- Take a side of the car each and stick the notes side-by-side gradually covering the surface.

- Get Little Miss Perfect to go and tell him what has happened. Hide in a place where you can see his reaction. He'll laugh, cry or steam with anger – but whatever he does, it'll be priceless

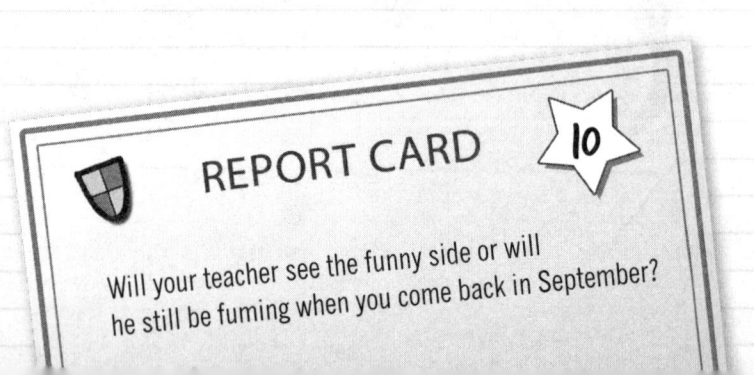

REPORT CARD 10

Will your teacher see the funny side or will he still be fuming when you come back in September?

107

Finger in a Cup

Who is the most squeamish in your class? Little Miss Perfect? The Swot? Or maybe the shy girl who hasn't spoken for three years? Whoever it is, you'd better leave them out of this one – it's so shocking they could faint. You are about to present a classmate with a bloody finger. It's a finger you have accidentally chopped off but have saved in a cup and are on the way to hospital to have sewn on again.

- You will need: a paper cup, some ketchup, some scissors and some cotton wool – and a finger!

- Take the scissors and cut a small hole in the base of the cup.

- Take some of the cotton wool and place it in the bottom of the cup around the hole.

- Splash some ketchup onto the cotton wool.

- Push your middle finger through the hole in the cup.

- Approach your victim and relate the terrible accident that happened. Now show them the bloody finger, keeping it perfectly still.

- If they still haven't completely freaked out, give your finger a little wiggle as if it is coming alive!

REPORT CARD 9

If you can pull off this truly horrifying prank, they'll hear the screams in the next class!

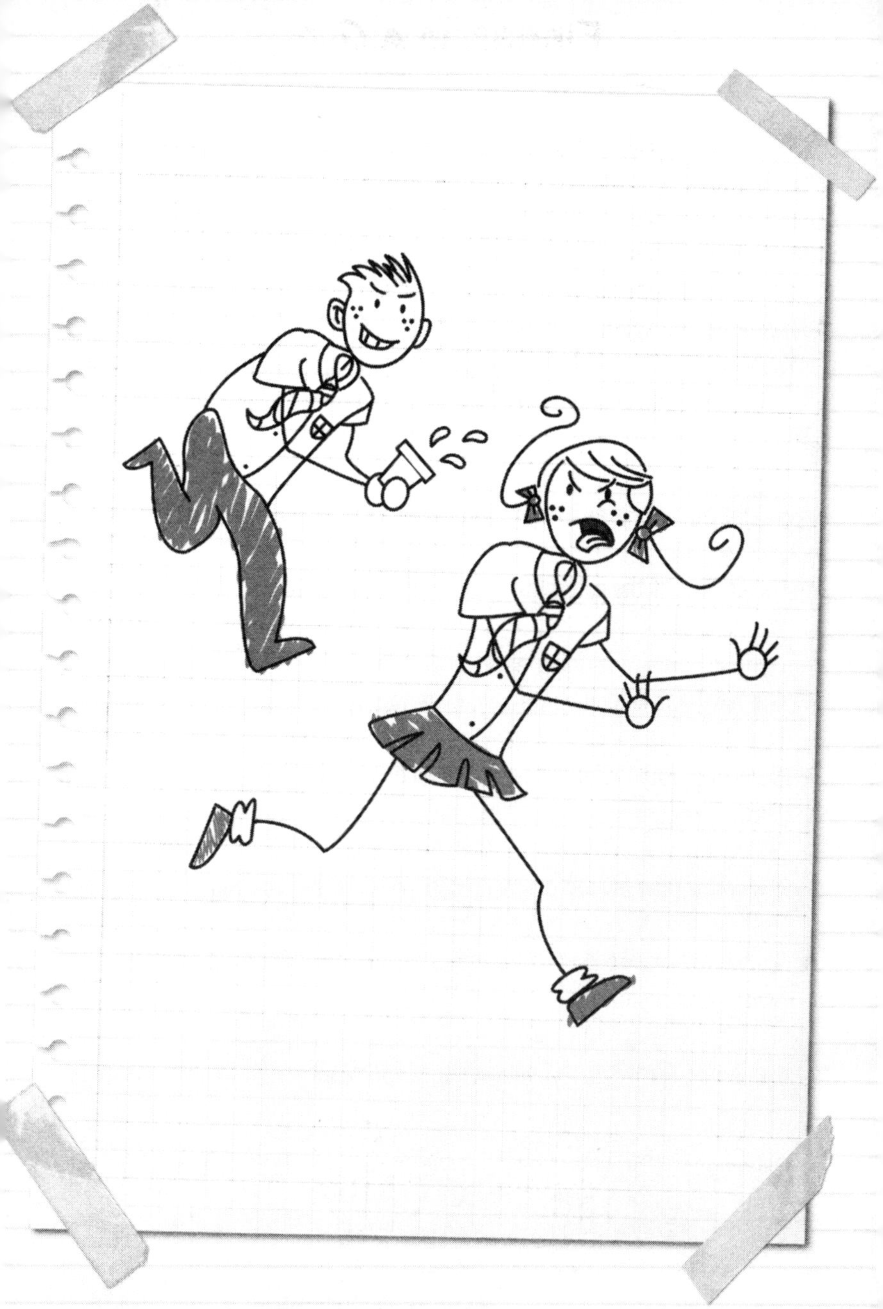

Shoelacing!

Sometimes you need a practical joke that is quick and easy — maybe as a means of getting revenge after you have been pranked yourself. In this case, look no further than the old-fashioned shoelace trick. Tying someone's shoelaces together isn't big or clever — but it can be a whole lot of fun.

A lot of kids wear velcro fasteners on their trainers and shoes — these can work just as well, but you have to be careful when you are undoing them — as well as feeling your hands at work they might hear the sound of the velcro being 'torn' open.

If you find you are being caught in the act of 'shoelacing' too often consider using cable ties — those small pieces of wire that are used to close food bags. These can be fixed by just a quick twist and can be just as effective.

- Try to match up the most inappropriate people possible. Your rival and The Swot, Little Miss Perfect and the messiest boy in class etc.

- Work as a team and see how many shoes you can tie together. Can you get a whole row?

- If you can't tie them to each other fix their laces to the chair or table legs.

- A great alternative is tying backpack straps together, while they are wearing them!

- And remember — once you have them tied together. Get them to run — it's so much funnier.

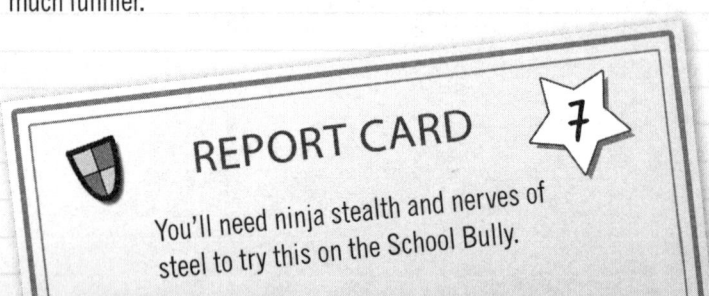

REPORT CARD 7

You'll need ninja stealth and nerves of steel to try this on the School Bully.

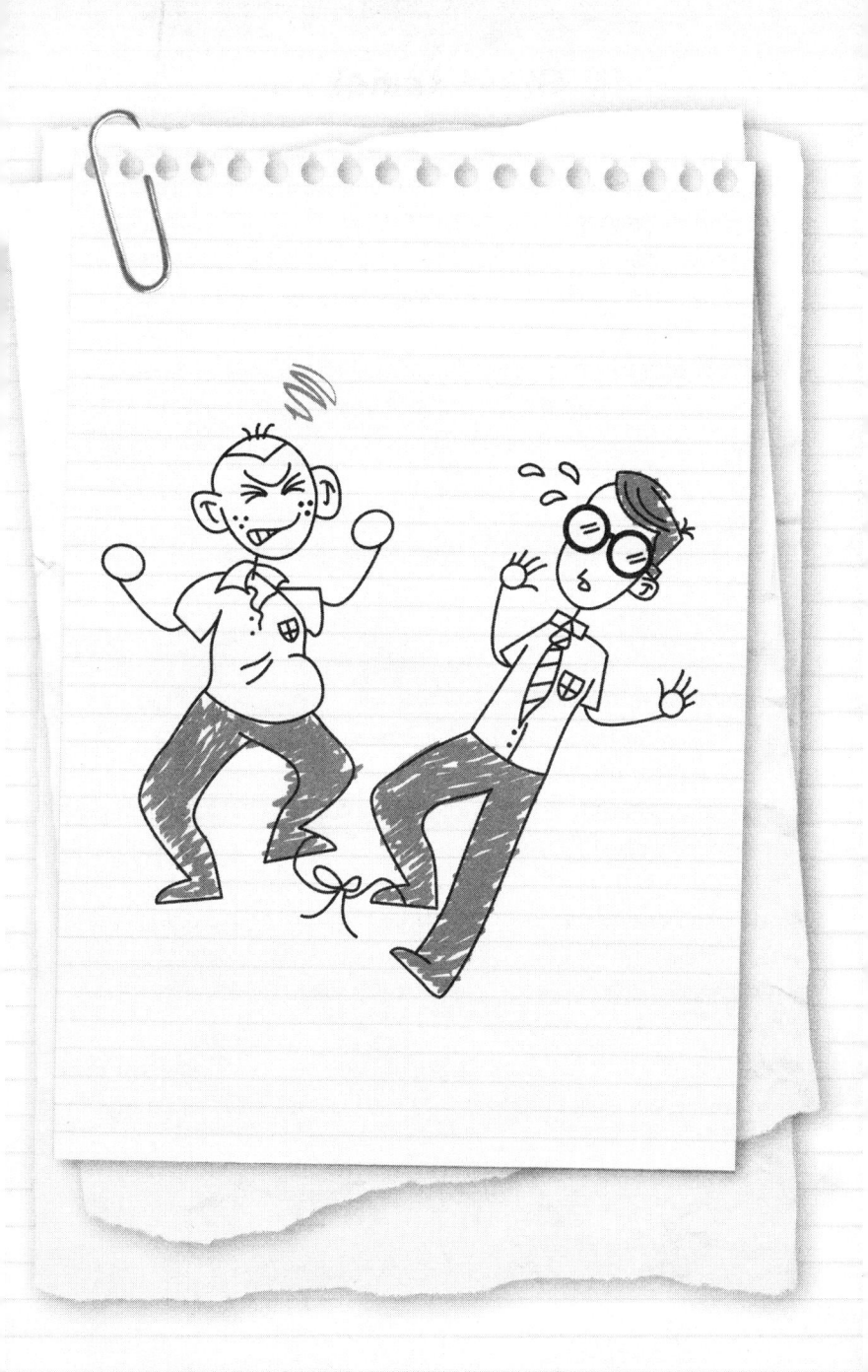

Snake in the Class

Who's afraid of a fake creepy crawly? Surely no one's fallen for that trick since year two. But if you make a plastic creature move, you can still make a fair few kids – and adults – scream!

- Find a scary-looking rubber or plastic snake. The more life-like it looks the more chance the prank will work.

- You'll need some see-through fishing line or if you can't get any you can try some white cotton.

- Tie the line around the neck of your snake and allow yourself a 'lead' of a metre or so.

- Hide the snake where it won't be found by accident. Under a bag or in a cupboard.

- Pick your moment and jerk your end of the snake's lead. The sudden movement should catch the eye of anyone nearby and, hopefully, make him or her jump out of their skin.

- Once you've perfected the trick, take your pet snake out of the classroom to torment music teachers, playground walkers, dinner ladies etc. And just imagine the havoc you could create in assembly!

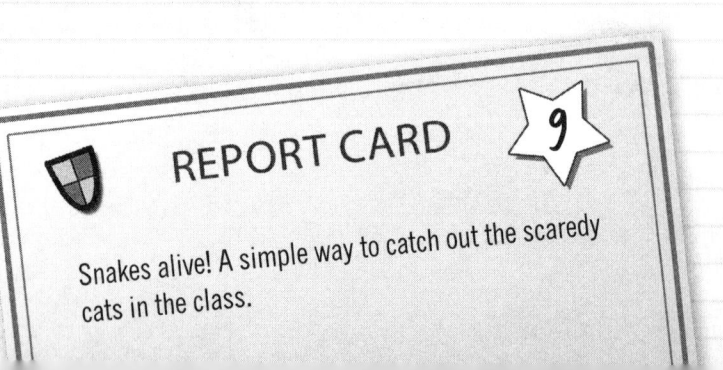

REPORT CARD ★9

Snakes alive! A simple way to catch out the scaredy cats in the class.

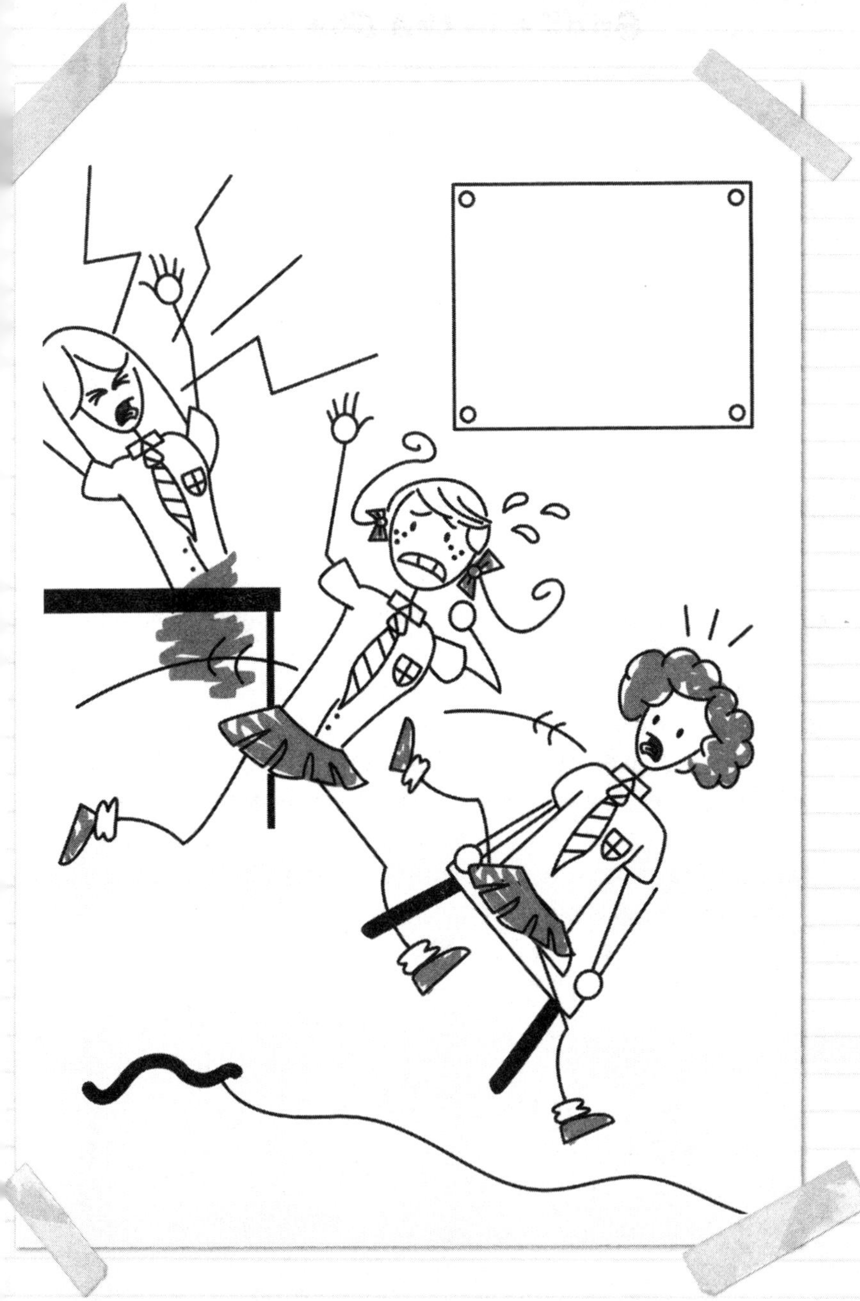

Squirty Time

No children's book would be complete without a suggestion for an art project. I'd hate to disappoint my readers so here it is. Naturally, it's a crafty kind of craft project for artistic pranksters.

- All you need is an empty old washing-up liquid bottle and a length of white string.

- Unscrew the cap from the bottle and thread the string through the hole at the top.

- Tie a knot at both ends of the string.

- Tuck the string all the way into the bottle until the top knot reaches the hole in the cap and can go no further.

- Now screw the cap back on and get ready to wreak havoc.

Everyone at school will be convinced that you really have a bottle full of soapy liquid — and you really don't need to tell them that you don't. When you finally squirt it, watch them run — the string really does look like soap shooting out the bottle. One you've fired, just stuff the string back into the bottle and go and find another new victim.

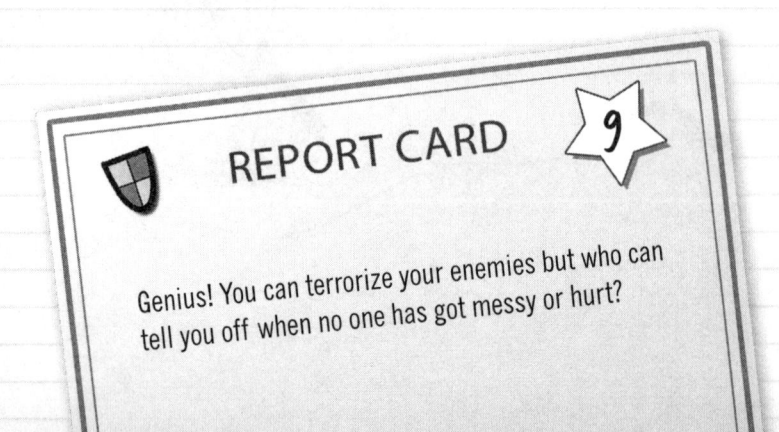

REPORT CARD 9

Genius! You can terrorize your enemies but who can tell you off when no one has got messy or hurt?

115

Table of Water

Some paper cups with some water – what's the big deal? I hear you say. Well, it may seem simple, but this is the kind of prank that can turn a teacher crimson with anger, make him tremble with frustration – and of course, end up making your life a nightmare. Is it worth it? I leave that up to you...

- You'll need your classmates help, so pick a time when your teacher has been mean to the whole class.

- Wait until you are all leaving the classroom for the day – maybe on a trip or a sports day or even at the end of school.

- Hand out two or three paper cups to everyone in the class. The more kids who join in, the less likely you are to be punished.

- Each of them needs to fill their cups with water (the fuller the better) and leave them on the teacher's desk.

- When your teacher returns to the class, he'll find a hundred cups of water on his desk. With no kids around he'll have to empty every single one of them himself – that's about 30 trips to the sink.

Now if you want to be really clever you can fill some of the cups with juice and spell out a message on the table. Keep it simple like "See ya!" or "Love 4B" – I'm sure your teacher will just love your creativity!

REPORT CARD 7

It's nice for the whole class to do a prank together – but boy are you all going to be in trouble when you see your teacher next.

117

The Magic Word

Why's your teacher got that quizzical look on her face? She's been "floccinaucinihilipilificated!"

You say "Flok-ina-sin-hili-pili-fi-cated," it means to make something seem worthless and it's one of the longest words in the English Language. Imagine if you used that when your teacher tells you to stop arguing with your friend? "But Sir, he's trying to floccinaucinihilipilificate me!"

OK. That might be difficult to remember but you can still have fun with words. When your teacher isn't around, get the whole class to agree on word. Not just any word, but one she wouldn't expect you to use or one that just sounds funny. Here's a couple of ideas but you can find your own...

- Aardvark (it's a burrowing mammal)
- Pickle (a confusion as in "he's in a right pickle" or a savoury jam)
- Lugubrious (means gloomy)

Everyone should use the word whenever they can through the day. When you ask questions, if you are answering the teacher's questions or when you're writing in your class books. Choose a scorekeeper and see who has used the word the most by the end of the day.

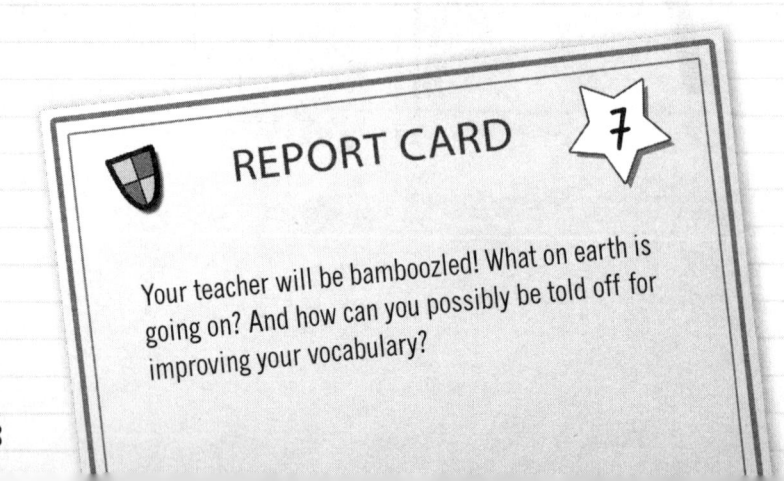

REPORT CARD 7

Your teacher will be bamboozled! What on earth is going on? And how can you possibly be told off for improving your vocabulary?

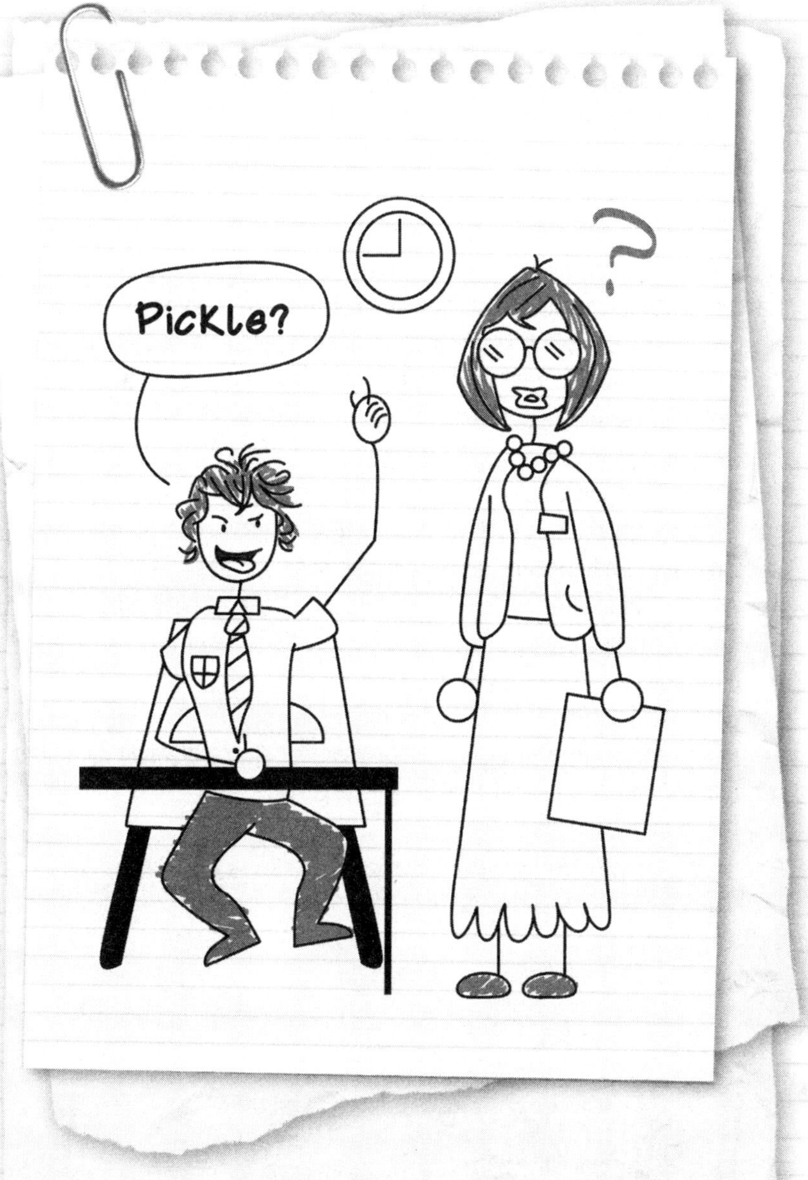
Pickle?

The Name Switch

"Jack?" "No Miss."

"Josh?" "Nope."

"Err... Jamal?"

Life's so tough for a supply teacher. A new school, a classroom you've never been in before and a set of kids you've never seen before. We really should give them a helping hand, shouldn't we? You mean prank them? No, that's cruel … it's really too mean – ok, perhaps just a harmless prank.

The first thing a supply teacher has to do is learn the name of everyone in the class. It's a pretty difficult thing to remember 30 names in half-an-hour – but you can make it that little bit harder and have some fun along the way.

When asked to say their names, the whole class should say the name of the person sitting next to them instead.

Try to remember to answer to that name, whenever she calls you. It'll give the whole prank away if you both start answering at once.

After lunch, confuse her even more by swapping back to your real name. If she doesn't believe you, show her your homework book. If she accuses you of trying to trick her, deny it and sympathetically say, "Oh, it must be so hard trying to remember all those names, Miss."

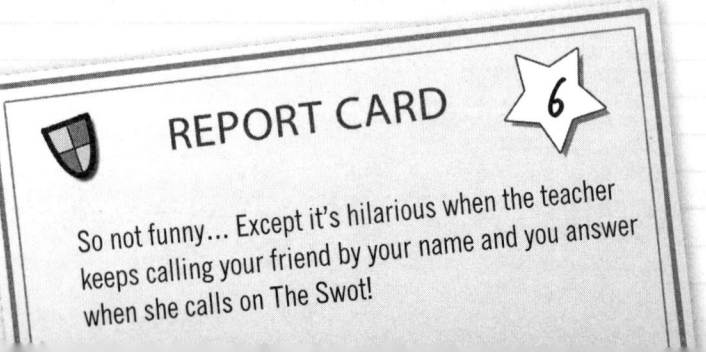

REPORT CARD ⭐ 6

So not funny... Except it's hilarious when the teacher keeps calling your friend by your name and you answer when she calls on The Swot!

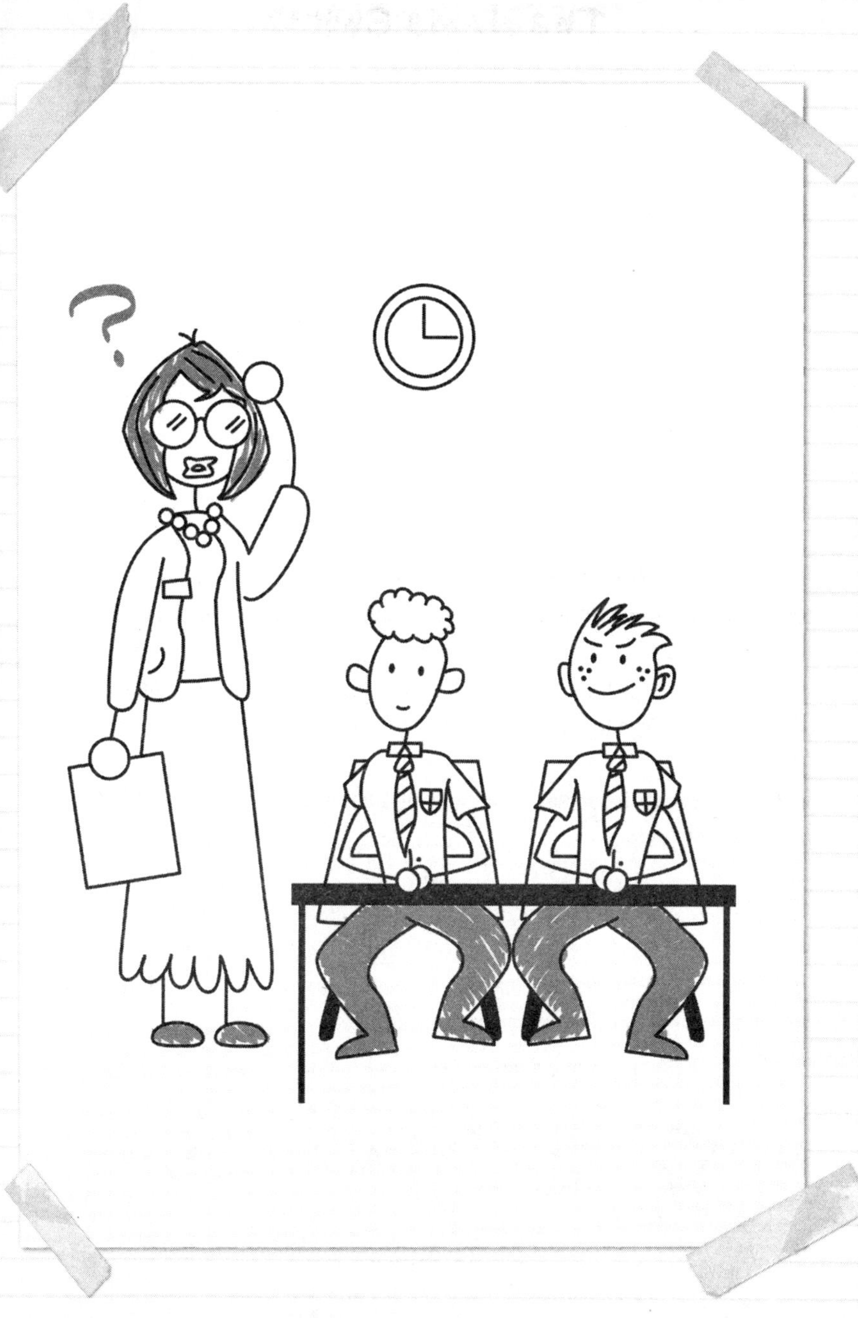

The Sound of Music

It starts with a low moaning sound that you can hardly hear. Then it slowly gets louder. There could be a loud wasp loose in the classroom, maybe the air conditioning is playing up or possibly the 4C choir are finding their voice again.

You need someone brave (and musical) and willing to start off the prank. He should wait until the teacher's back is turned before quietly beginning to hum. He can hum a proper tune or even more annoyingly just start a steady note, but he needs to keep his mouth firmly closed while he does so.

If the teacher notices him let the hummer go silent as long as someone else takes up the 'tune' immediately.

After about ten seconds, someone else needs to join in. It should be loud enough for the back of the class to hear but not quite loud enough for the teacher to catch on.

Now more friends need to join in, with the humming getting louder and louder.

If the teacher turns around, everyone stop immediately. As soon as he turns back, start up again.

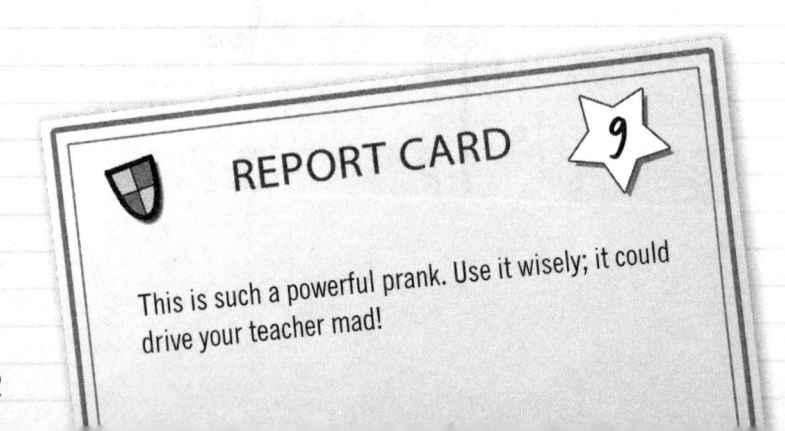

REPORT CARD ⭐ 9

This is such a powerful prank. Use it wisely; it could drive your teacher mad!

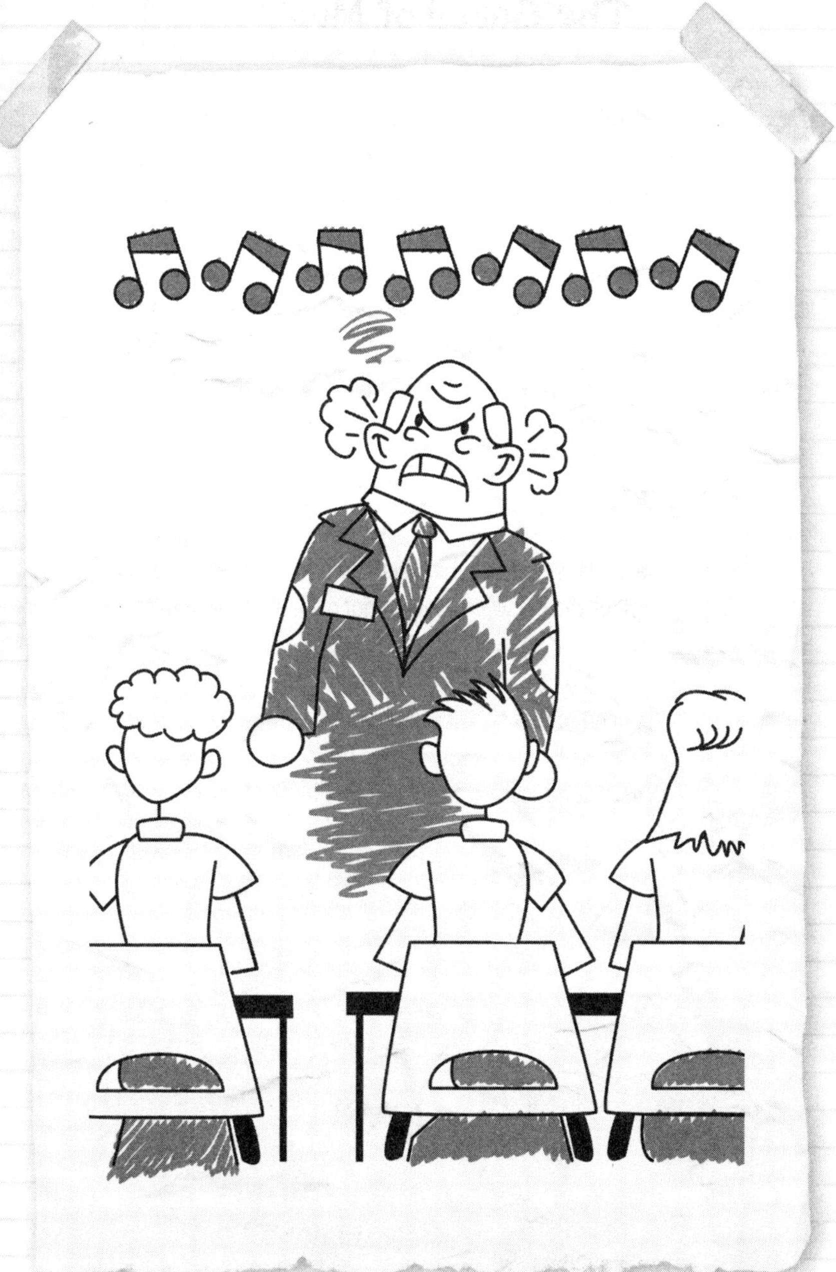

Minty Teeth

Ever noticed how similar some small mint sweets are to your teeth? They seem to be begging to be used in a prank. If only we knew someone with a wicked sense of humour who thinks that pretending to lose his or her teeth can be funny?

- Want to have a break during a boring lesson? Secretly pop a mint into your mouth, stick your hand up and tell the teacher you think your tooth is a little loose. Show just how brave you are by reaching in and yanking the 'tooth' out of your mouth. If you're feeling really brave, repeat the trick with a second tooth ten minutes later!

- When the teacher on lunch duty asks you why you haven't eaten your dinner tell them you thought the chicken was too tough. Then prove it by spitting out three 'teeth' that have come loose while you've been chewing it.

- "Fight! Fight!" You and your best friend seem to have fallen out. He's got a grip on you and has (pretended to) hit you in the face. Almost in tears, you put your hand to your mouth and retrieve three 'teeth'. A quick bite of a sachet of ketchup while you are tussling will produce some 'blood' to make it even more realistic.

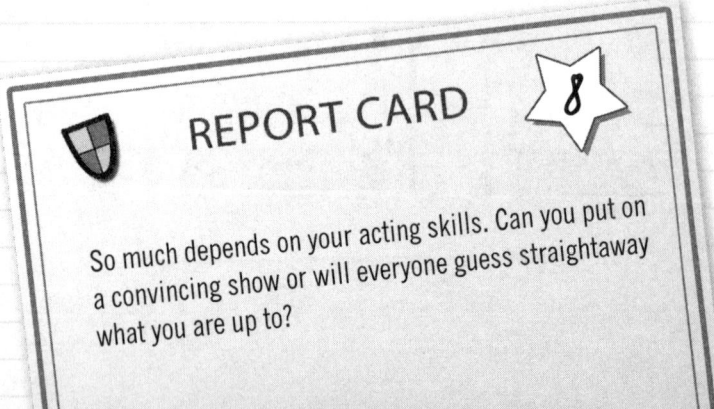

REPORT CARD

So much depends on your acting skills. Can you put on a convincing show or will everyone guess straightaway what you are up to?

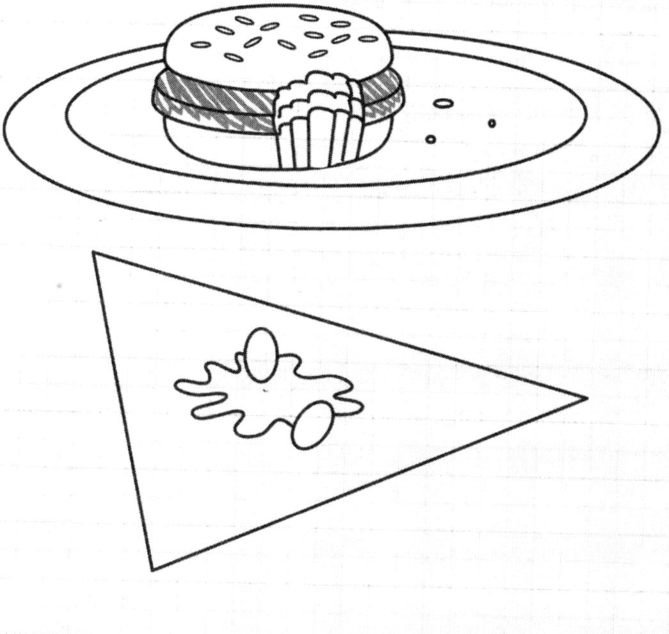

Timber!

Registration. Every class in every school does it, but it's a bit dull isn't it? Every morning the same names are called out with the same bored replies of "Here" or "Yes". Isn't it time we livened things up a little?

- Make sure at least half of your class are in on the prank and whoever is last on the register (Zabrisky? Zebedee? Zachariah?) knows exactly what they have to do.

- When the teacher calls out your name instead of saying "Here", you shout "Chop".

- If enough people join in it will sound like someone is chopping a tree down. "Chop, Chop, Chop!"

- The last person on the register gets to do the final shout of "Timber!!!"

- At this call – all the class fall of their chairs at the same time.

- If the teacher gets sick of you doing this change the game to 'The Bomb'. Now in turn you reply "Tick!" and "Tock" – this time the last on the list will shout "Booom!" and you all jump in the air.

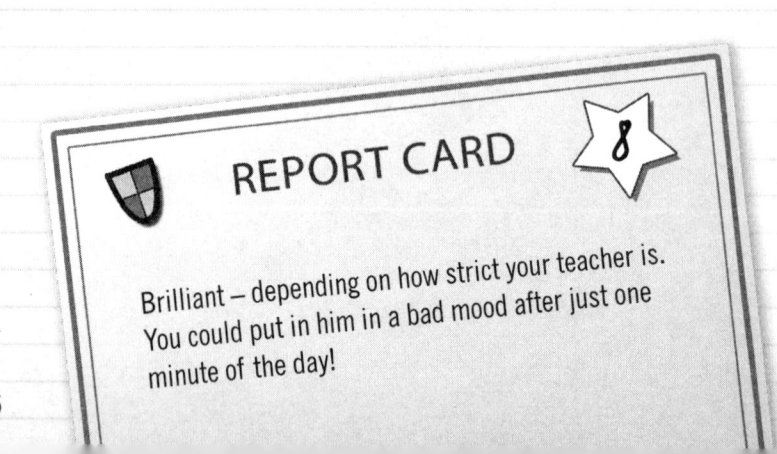

REPORT CARD — 8

Brilliant – depending on how strict your teacher is. You could put in him in a bad mood after just one minute of the day!

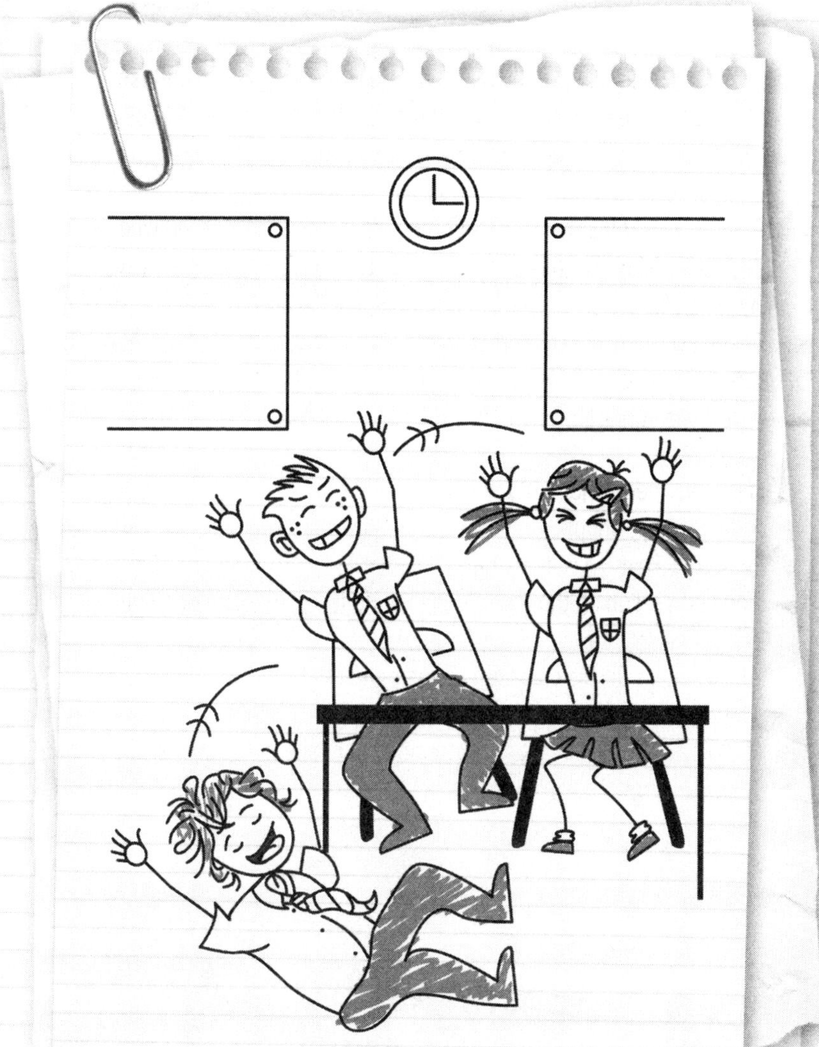

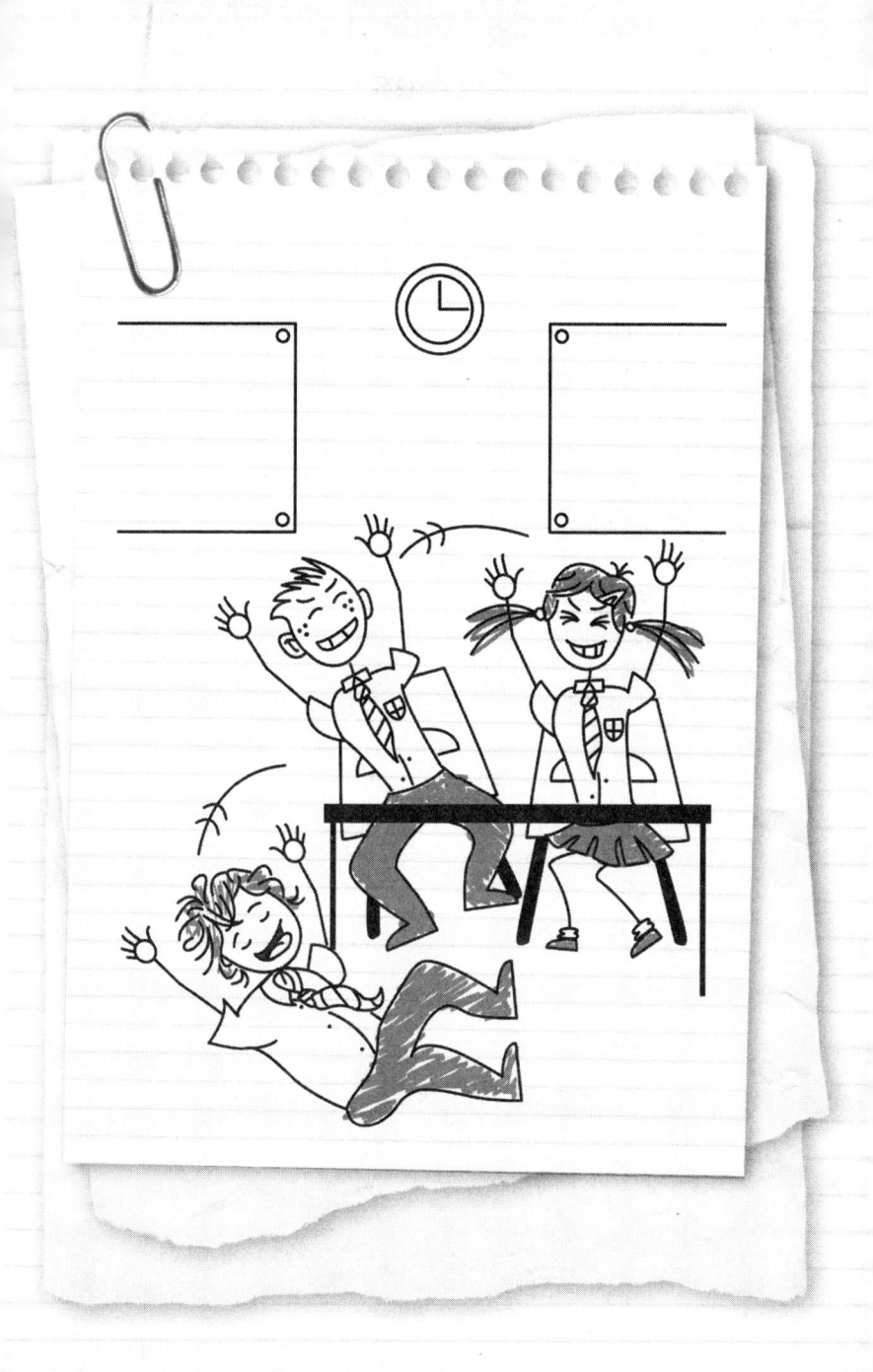

Kick Me!

This one is so old it was even being played by Stone Age children! Simply write "Kick Me" on a post-it note and attach it to someone's back without them knowing (it was much more difficult for Stone Age kids. They had to draw a picture on a rock and try to stick that to the victim's bear skin jumper!). All day they'll find themselves being kicked up the backside with no idea why.

The only difficult part is attaching the note. The best method is to slap them on the back in a friendly way, saying something like "I like you, we should be good friends". They'll be suspicious but won't realize just what you have done.

All good fun, but a master prankster won't be happy with just getting someone kicked. Is there something more fun you can write like...

"I can fart at will – just ask me."

"I've just farted – smell my bum!"

"I've got sweets for everybody."

Or even...

"Kiss me quick."

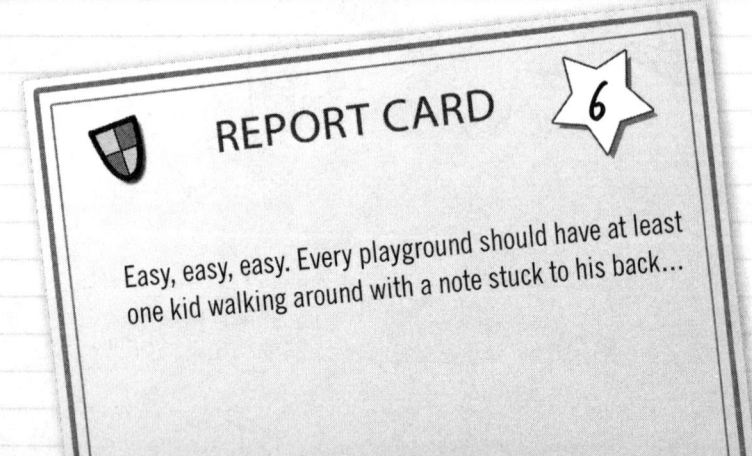

REPORT CARD 6

Easy, easy, easy. Every playground should have at least one kid walking around with a note stuck to his back...

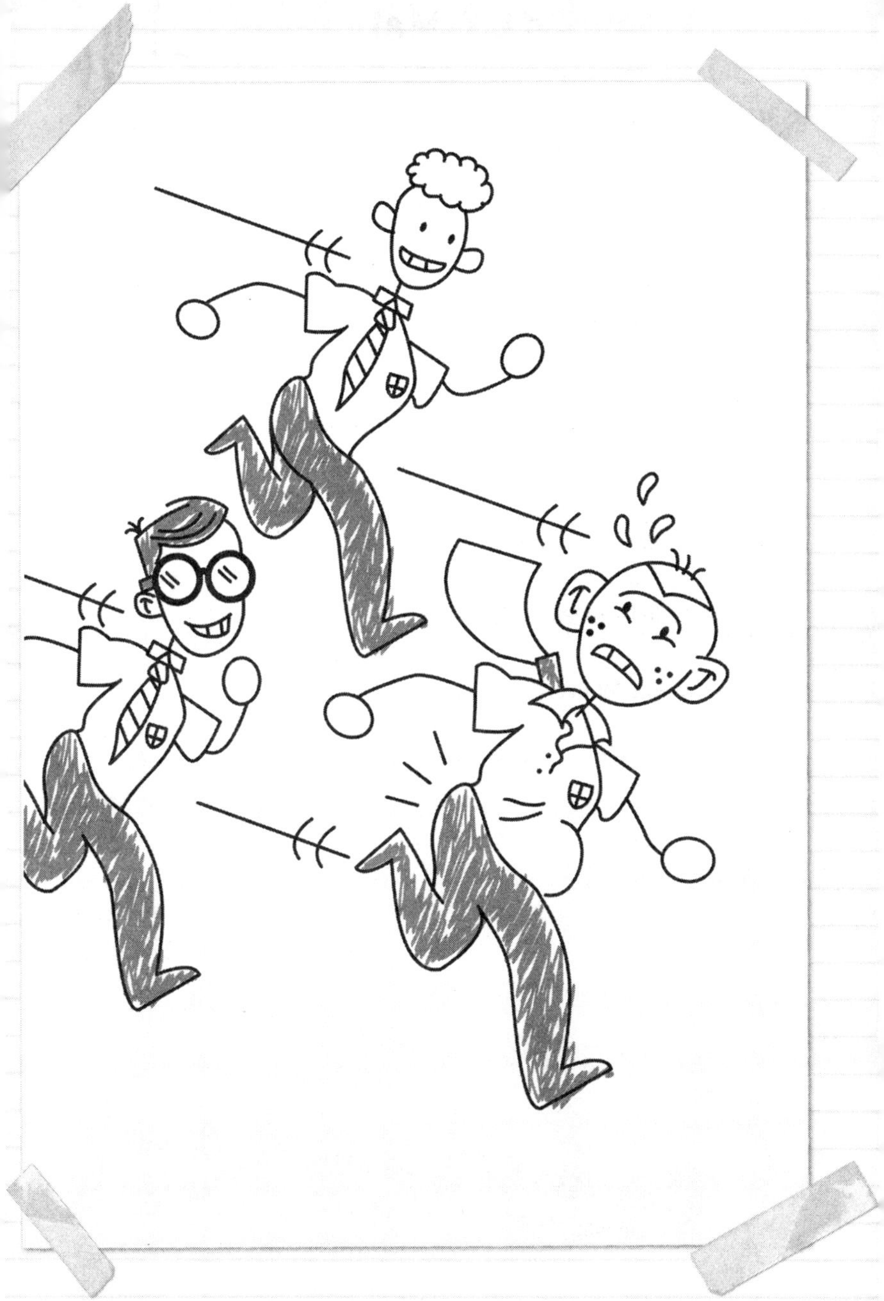

Yum, Yum, Wiggly Worm!

How far would you go to shock your classmates? How about taking a bite out of an earthworm? A slimy, oozing-with-mud worm from the garden that is still wriggling when it is inside your mouth?

Hang on! Stop digging and come back. You don't have to actually eat a real live worm. There are some pretty realistic – and tasty – gummy worms available at the sweet shop.

- Buy a packet of gummy worms and take out the black and red ones – these look most like the real thing. Now think of some situations where you might find a real worm...

- A piece of lettuce with your lunch? Wouldn't it be terrible if a 'worm' had crawled in? Oh no! You hadn't noticed and you've bitten it in half!

- Gone to collect the ball from the school garden? What's that you've (pretended to have) found in the mud? You're not going to, are you? Yuccck!

- Make a small hole in an apple with a pen. Poke your gummy worm into the hole until just its head is sticking out. After lunch take out your apple and take a bite from the opposite side. When everyone screams, you can calmly say "Oh, what a treat! And take a bite of apple and worm together. "Delicious"!

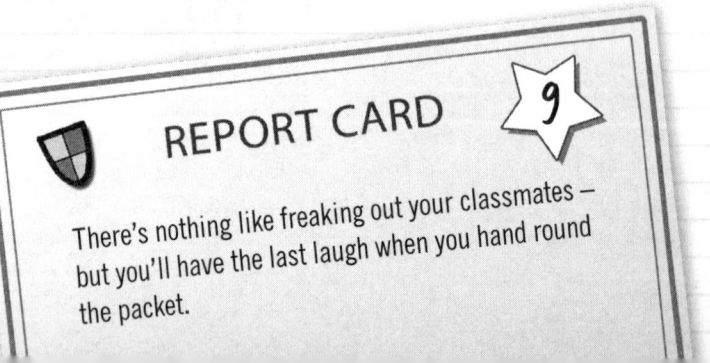

REPORT CARD 9

There's nothing like freaking out your classmates – but you'll have the last laugh when you hand round the packet.

You Spilled What?

What's your homework book look like? I bet it's full of crossings out, doodles and scribbles. The cover is probably dogged-eared (even dog-nibbled) and there's sure to be bits of your tea sticking the pages together (Hmm... half a baked-bean!). Little Miss Perfect's book, on the other hand, is a work of art. Her name adorned with flowers, her handwriting neat and every page looking brand new. Wouldn't it be awful if she thought you'd spilled something on it?

Luckily, you can make a trick 'spillage' that will totally fool her — and then take it away before you even get in any trouble. Perfect...

- Ask your mum for an old bottle of nail polish that she doesn't want anymore (you're doing yet another science experiment!).

- Unscrew the top and pour it out on to a piece of greaseproof kitchen paper so it creates a small puddle.

- Leave it until it has dried completely then peel it off of the paper.

- Now you have your own spillage you can sneakily place anywhere you like. Depending on the colour it might look like ketchup, brown sauce, blood or something even more yucky!

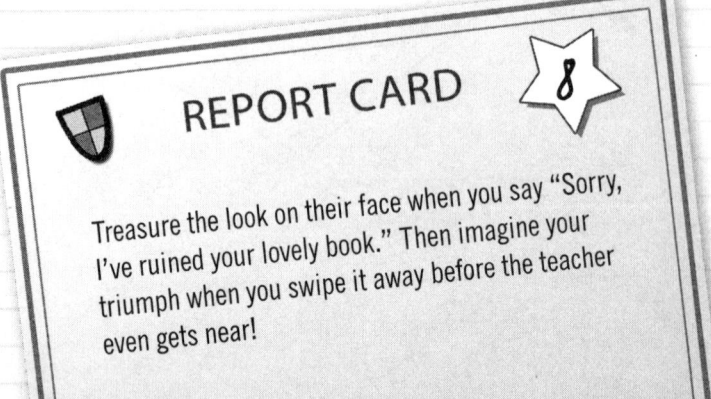

REPORT CARD

Treasure the look on their face when you say "Sorry, I've ruined your lovely book." Then imagine your triumph when you swipe it away before the teacher even gets near!

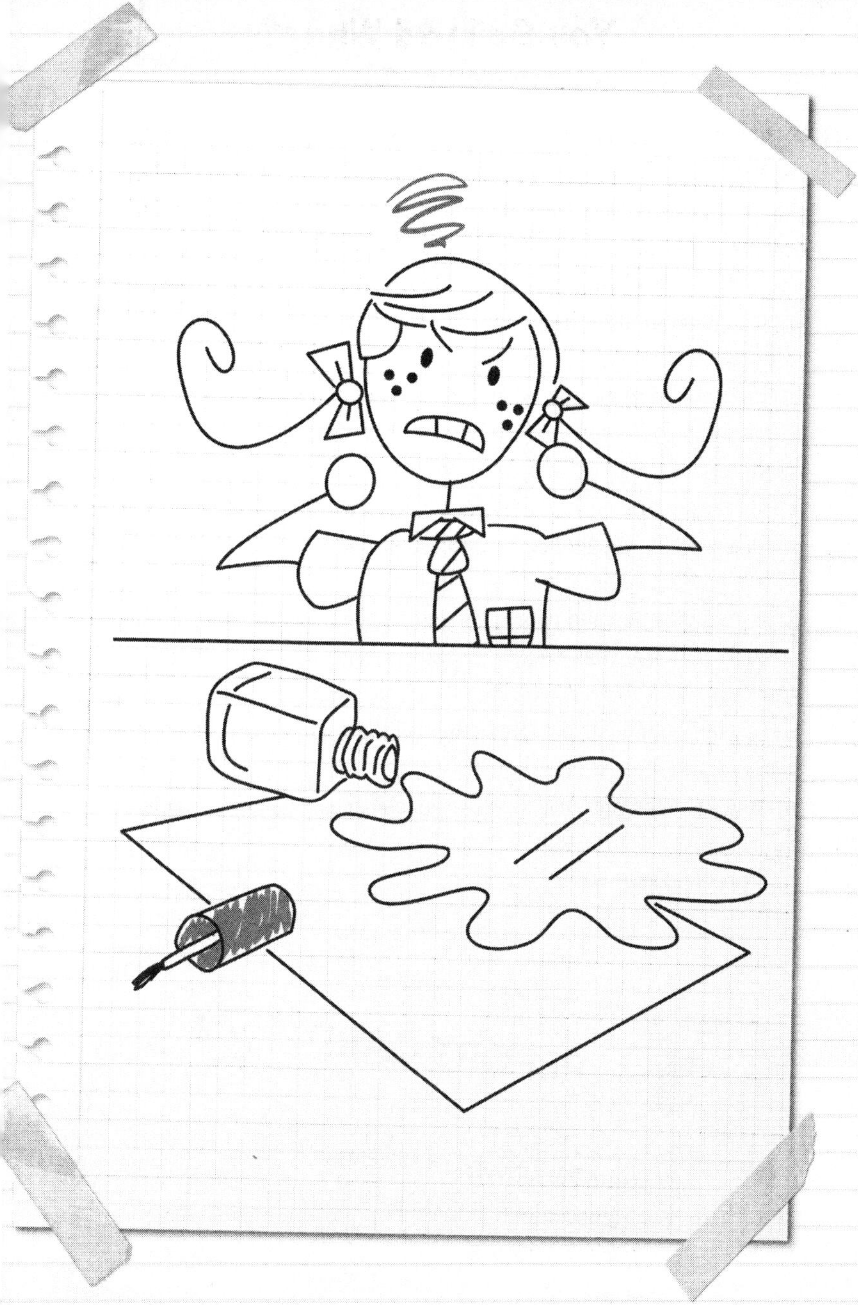

Your Shoes Are Too Small

It's time for PE. Mr Popular has changed from his gleaming shoes into his spotless white super-trainers. He's won the running races, scored a hat-trick in the football and even beaten the girls at skipping. And now you're going to have to listen to him going on and on about it for hours and hours. But wait a second... what's happened here? He can't get his shoes back on. Super Prankster (Hello? Wake up! That's you!) has saved the day. Here's how...

- Wait for him to go into the hall or the gym for PE.

- Be ready with a fistful of (clean) scrunched-up toilet paper.

- Shove the toilet paper as far as you can towards the toes of his shoes.

- Replace the shoes in exactly the same position as you found them.

When he goes to change back into his shoes, he'll discover that somehow – in the space of half-an-hour – they have shrunk and no longer fit him. The more he tries to ram his toes to the bottom, the more the paper will be jammed into the toes. You'll be half way through the next lesson before he realises what has happened.

REPORT CARD

The simplest pranks are the best! For a really impressive prank try 'shrinking' the whole classes shoes. Remember, of course, that this won't work with open-toed sandals. If you do this well, there's a high chance you'll be in hysterics – so make sure you don't split your trousers when you're laughing!

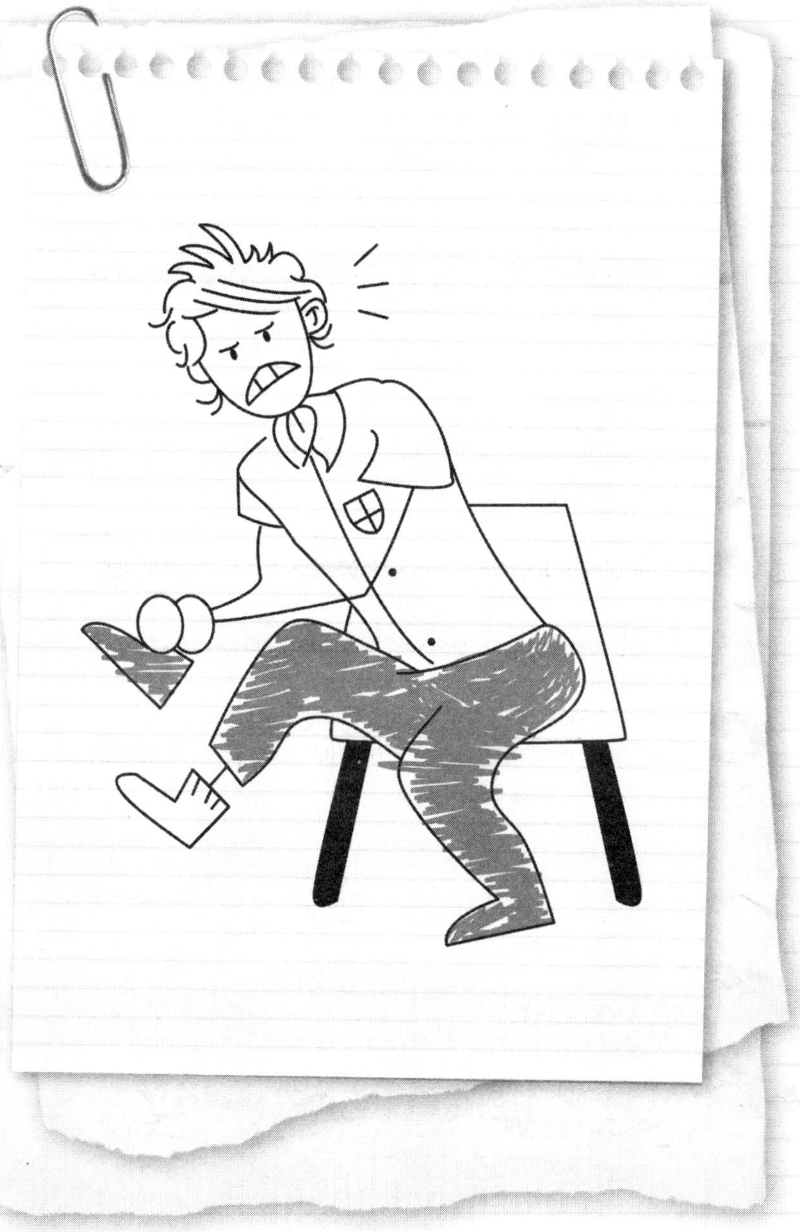

Cactus Friend

Do the rest of your class think you're barking mad? Well, they will do after you've performed this prank. You are going to pretend you have a friend who's a plant. Yep – you read that right. A plant.

- Get yourself a small cactus plant. They can be bought very cheaply at school fairs and garden centres and take absolutely no looking after.

- Take your cactus into class with you. Put it on your desk but don't pay any attention to it.

- During a lesson raise your hand and when asked tell the teacher that the cactus has a question.

- Look at the cactus and wait as if it is going to say something.

- Obviously it won't say anything, so shrug disappointedly and say "sorry" to the teacher.

- Later in the day do the same thing a couple more times. Each time, you need to get a little angrier with your plant friend.

- Finally, when school ends for the day, pick up the cactus and shout, "I can't believe you embarrassed me again. You're never coming with me again!"

REPORT CARD 6

Could go either way this one. Everyone will think it's cool and the teacher will see the funny side... or your parents could be getting a call to get your head examined!

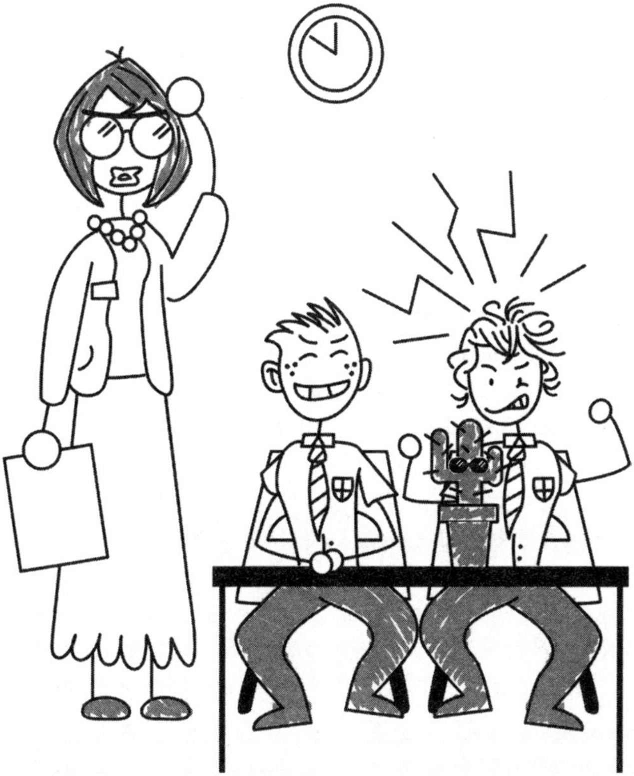

Binocular Eyes

Curiosity is the prankster's friend. Seeing your victim walk right into your trap makes it all the funnier. After all, no one asked them to look through your binoculars – maybe you could have warned them, but they were so keen you didn't want to disappoint them...

- Take a pair of binoculars and some dark eye-shadow (avoid getting in even more trouble by asking your mum if you can borrow some – you can explain that it's for yet another special science experiment).

- Apply a small amount of the make-up around the eyepieces of the binoculars.

- At break take your position near your chosen victim.

- Pretend to look through the binoculars, but remember not to put your eyes to the eyepieces or you'll be the one everyone is laughing at.

- Make some excited noises – "Cor! Look at that!" or "A-may-zing!" – and wait for your victim to ask to have a look through them.

- Hand them to your victim and point out something for them to look at in the distance.

- When they take off the binoculars they'll have dark circles around their eyes. See how long it takes them to find out and work out where they came from!

REPORT CARD

9

Guaranteed prank value – but how many black eyes can you give before your classmates work out that you are the culprit?

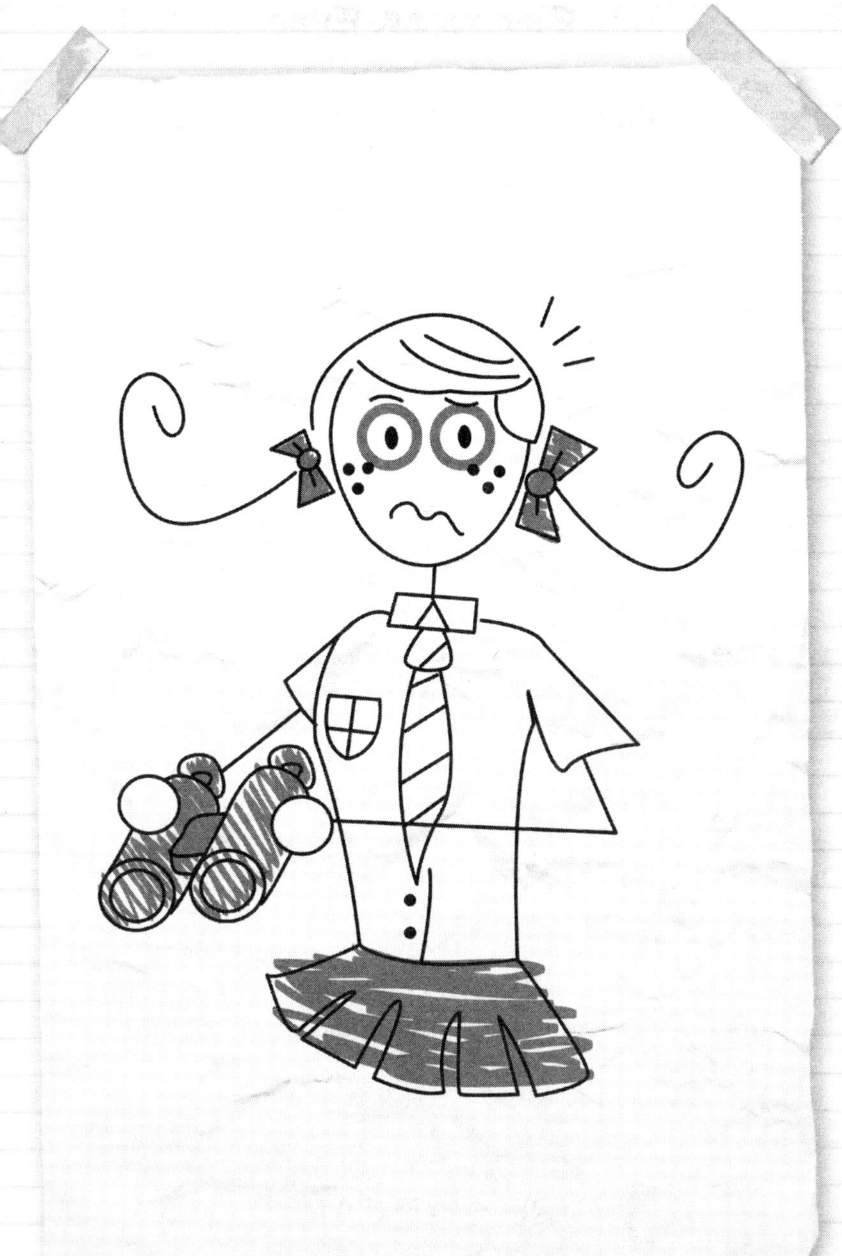

This Takes the Biscuit

What better way to apologise for all the pranks you've pulled than to hand out some delicious biscuits? And what better way to have another great laugh than to give them yet another mouth-watering surprise?

- Buy a packet of biscuits. You'll need the 'sandwich' type such as custard creams

- Open the packet and take out all the biscuits.

- Carefully separate each side of the 'sandwich' and scrape out the filling.

- Take a tube of toothpaste and spread a little on each biscuit.

- Remake the biscuit sandwiches and put them in a tin.

Now come up with a good story to explain why you are taking biscuits into school. Everyone will know it's not the kind of thing you do and be very suspicious unless you say – "My mum is going on a diet and doesn't want then in the house" or "My little brother is allergic to them." Then, working fast – before they realize what's inside – offer them around to your classmates. Count to three and wait for the reaction...

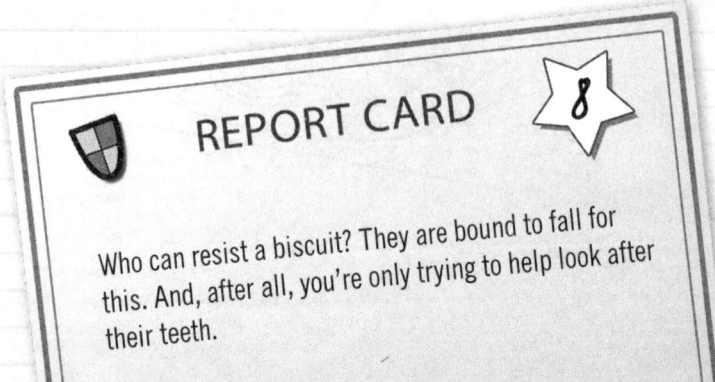

REPORT CARD

Who can resist a biscuit? They are bound to fall for this. And, after all, you're only trying to help look after their teeth.

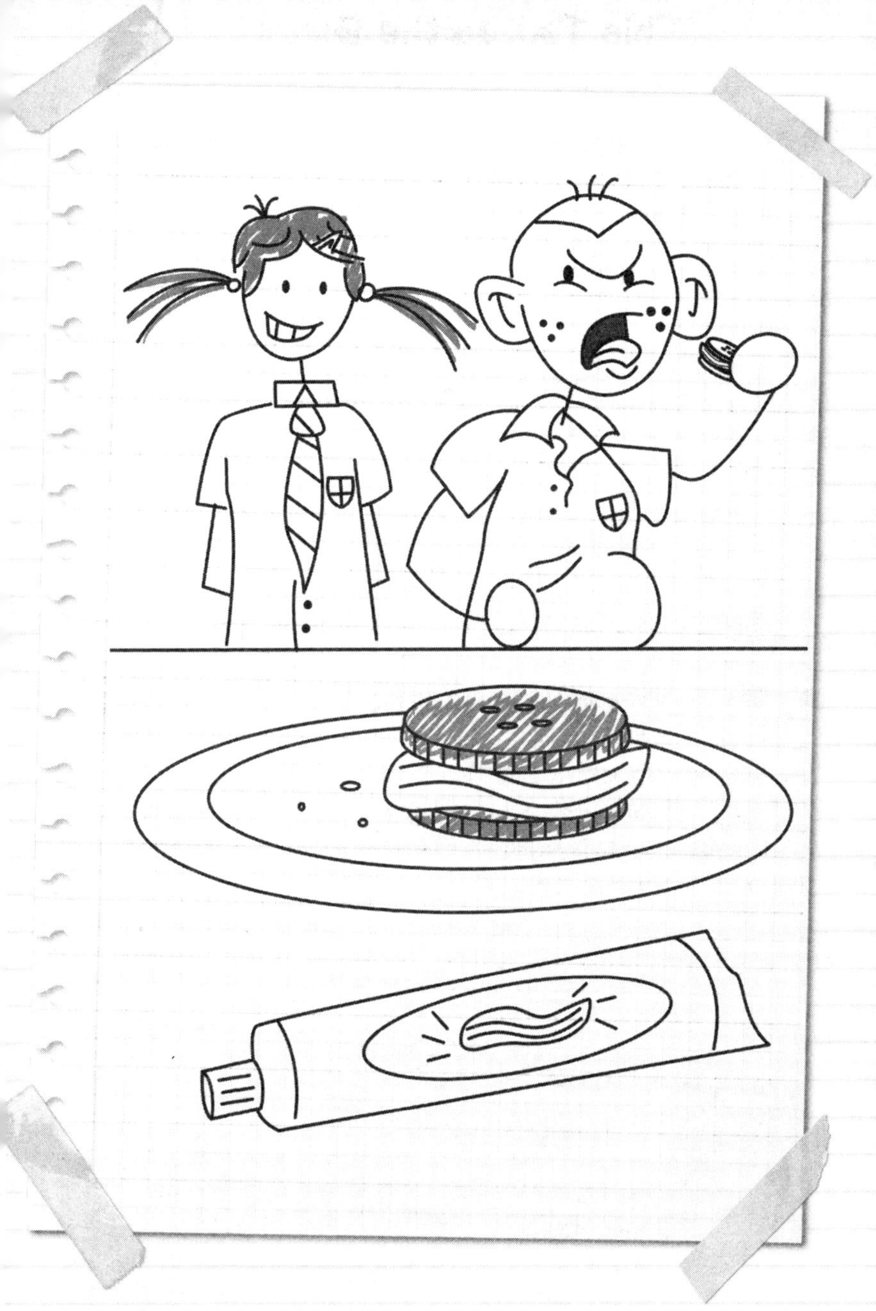

Chicken Run

This is so off-the dial fabulous, it could only be an end-of-term prank – when everyone's excited about summer and even the teachers are in such a good mood that they will let you off. Even better, if you are in year six and won't have to show your face in the school for a long time!

- You will need three chickens (told you this was off-the dial!) and some paper stickers.

- Write numbers '1', '2' and '4' on separate sheets of paper.

- Using the stickers, label each chicken with a different number.

- With some help from your friends, secretly release the chickens in the playground.

- Stand back and watch the mayhem begin.

The fun begins by watching the children and teachers charging around the playground trying to catch the chickens. This could go on for hours! However, once they have caught them your numbering will have them guessing... there must be a number three chicken? Where could it have got to? Now instead of trying to catch clucking, scurrying chickens, they will be searching for a chicken that doesn't exist!

REPORT CARD 10

Have you spotted the problem with this prank? Somehow you have to get the chickens home again – and this means confessing your crime. Just hope that end-of-term happy feeling has spread to the caretaker and the teachers!

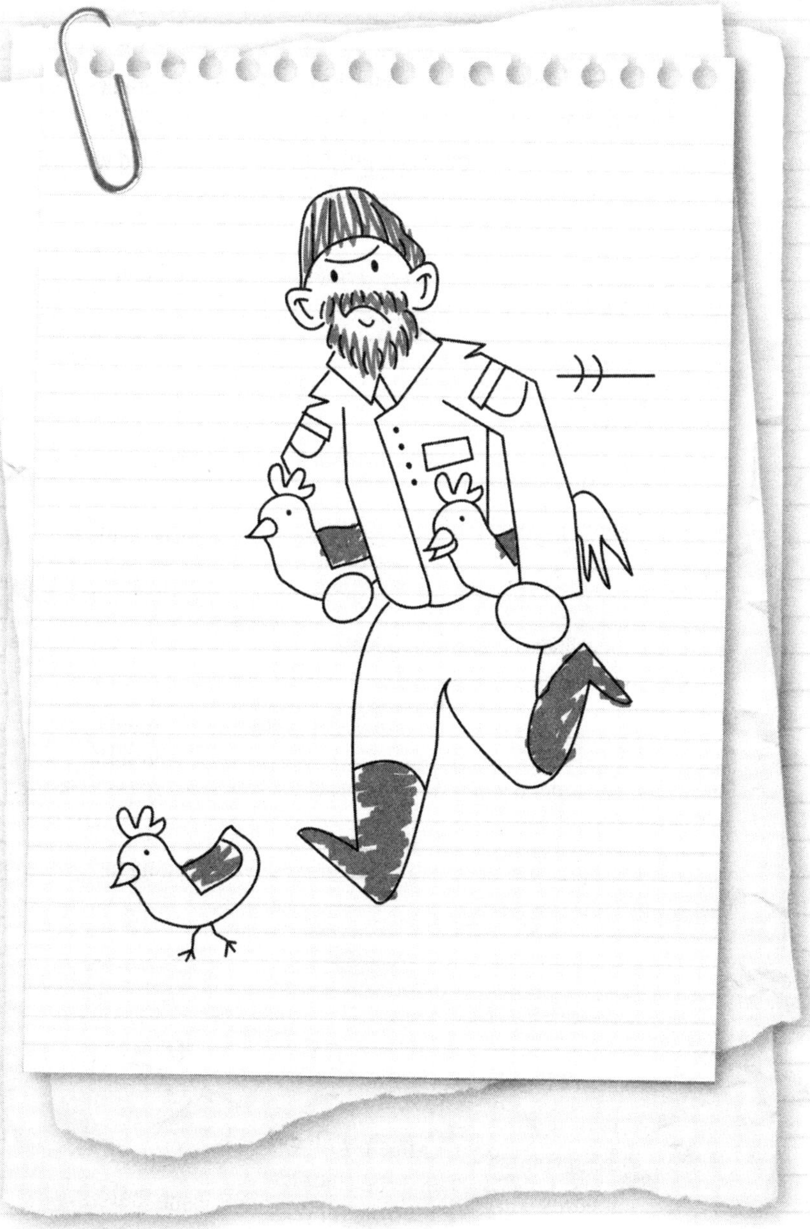

Prank Score Card

Date	Prank	Score

Grand Total: